Renegade Marketing Bible for Tree & Landscaping Professionals

99 Ways to Get More Clients in a Month Than You Get All Year

John P. Davis

authorHOUSE®

AuthorHouse™
1663 Liberty Drive, Suite 200
Bloomington, IN 47403
www.authorhouse.com
Phone: 1-800-839-8640

© 2008 John P. Davis. All rights reserved.

No part of this book may be reproduced, stored in a retrieval system, or transmitted by any means without the written permission of the author.

First published by AuthorHouse 4/29/2008

Printed in the United States of America
Bloomington, Indiana

This book is printed on acid-free paper.

ISBN: 978-1-4343-3353-7 (sc)

Library of Congress Control Number: 2007909409

Disclaimer

    This manual is designed to provide information in regard to the subject matter covered. It is sold with the understanding that the publisher and authors and advisers are not rendering legal, accounting, or other professional services.

    It is not the purpose of this manual to reprint all the information that is otherwise available to authors, printers, and publisher but to complement, amplify, and supplement other texts. For more information, see the references throughout the text. Every effort has been made to make this manual as complete and as accurate as possible.

    However, there may be mistakes, both typographical and in content. Therefore, this text should be used only as a general guide and not as the ultimate source of publishing information. Furthermore, this manual contains information only up to the printing date.

    The authors, advisers, and publisher shall have neither liability nor responsibility to any person or entity with respect to any loss or damage caused or alleged to be caused directly or indirectly by the information contained in this manual.

Contents

Introduction

Five Reasons Why Marketing Fails   xi

Section 1: First Things First

Know where you are—and where you are going   3
Strategy 1: Have a marketing plan   5
Strategy 2: Put numbers into the plan   7
Strategy 3: Develop your Unique Selling Proposition   10
Strategy 4: Set your pricing standards   13

Be a marketing expert   15
Strategy 5: Learn everything for yourself   16
Strategy 6: Constantly learn   17
Strategy 7: Attend industry meetings   18
Strategy 8: Read trade journals   19
Strategy 9: Learn by example   20
Strategy 10: "Steal" marketing ideas   21

Be a great manager   23
Strategy 11: Do something   24
Strategy 12: Be consistent   25
Strategy 13: Stay on top of things   27
Strategy 14: Get employees involved   28
Strategy 15: Keep employees informed and educated   30
Strategy 16: Motivate employees   31
Strategy 17: Get rid of "bad apple" customers   32
Strategy 18: Work on your business, not in your business   33

Be a leader — 34

Strategy 19: Use time in your vehicle to keep learning — 35
Strategy 20: Be professional — 36
Strategy 21: Model top-notch ethics — 38
Strategy 22: Hold yourself accountable — 40
Strategy 23: Remove mental garbage — 41
Strategy 24: Keep yourself motivated — 43
Strategy 25: Stay in tune with your clients, staff, and service — 44

Section 2: How to Make Big Things Happen

Marketing communications — 46

Strategy 26: Write copy that sells — 47
Strategy 27: Tape record yourself — 49
Strategy 28: Use direct-response marketing — 50
Strategy 29: Master direct mail — 53
Strategy 30: Use letters, not brochures — 55
Strategy 31: Use form letters and cards — 57
Strategy 32: Don't be boring! — 58
Strategy 33: Get in the newspaper — 59
Strategy 34: Write a book or report — 61
Strategy 35: Write a column — 63
Strategy 36: Get best use from the Yellow Pages — 65
Strategy 37: Use traveling billboards — 68
Strategy 38: Double your response from mailer services — 69
Strategy 39: Send out a newsletter — 70
Strategy 40: Advertise — 73
Strategy 41: Do you really believe folks keep your business card? — 74
Strategy 42: Don't be an advertising victim. — 77
Strategy 43: Master newspaper advertising — 79

Customer service — 81

Strategy 44: Understand the lifetime value of a client — 82
Strategy 45: They are clients, not customers — 84
Strategy 46: Remember that you are not the client — 85
Strategy 47: Wow your clients — 86
Strategy 48: Cater to your dream clients — 88
Strategy 49: Cater to your dream referral clients — 89
Strategy 50: Constantly educate your clients — 90
Strategy 51: Set up a lending library — 92
Strategy 52: Send thank-you letters — 94
Strategy 53: Give workshops — 96
Strategy 54: Give a big, bold, solid guarantee — 101
Strategy 55: Respond to complaints fast — 105
Strategy 56: Better your competition — 108
Strategy 57: Understand your clients' mindset — 112

Making new sales — 114

Strategy 58: Get a competitive edge by selling with pruning standards — 115
Strategy 59: Pay attention to the front end — 116
Strategy 60: Never leave them empty-handed — 118
Strategy 61: Require new prospects to meet with you when delivering a proposal — 120
Strategy 62: Let them choose between you, you, and you — 122
Strategy 63: Be a sales superstar, and love it! — 123
Strategy 64: Give evaluations, not estimates — 125
Strategy 65: Give FREE "Tree-Hazard Evaluations" — 126

Making more sales — 127

Strategy 66: Pay attention to the back end — 128
Strategy 67: Create a cash-flow surge — 129
Strategy 68: Up-sell and cross-sell — 132

Section 3: Systems to Make Things Happen

Processes and procedures that keep the marketing machine going — 135

- Strategy 69: Discover your "business DNA" — 136
- Strategy 70: Create a marketing system — 141
- Strategy 71: Keep a client database — 142
- Strategy 72: Create a sales system — 143
- Strategy 73: Keep a networking file — 144
- Strategy 74: Create a new-client or prospect kit — 146
- Strategy 75: Set up your voicemail to market for you — 148
- Strategy 76: Have a system for follow-up calls — 150
- Strategy 77: Conduct target farming — 152
- Strategy 78: Get and use testimonials — 155
- Strategy 79: How to get testimonials — 157
- Strategy 80: What testimonials should say — 158
- Strategy 81: Keep a book of testimonials — 159
- Strategy 82: Set up a referral program — 160
- Strategy 83: Reward your referrers — 162
- Strategy 84: Establish a monetary reward referral program — 163
- Strategy 85: Track referral sources — 165
- Strategy 86: Track your results — 166
- Strategy 87: Track clients and prospects — 168
- Strategy 88: Know your numbers — 169
- Strategy 89: Hold weekly meetings — 170
- Strategy 90: Test. And test. And test. — 172

Section 4: Growing the Business

Strategies to add in once you're really moving — 173

- Strategy 91: Raise your prices — 174
- Strategy 92: Add more services — 176
- Strategy 93: Diversify your market — 177

Strategy 94: Network 178
Strategy 95: Launch a charity program 179
Strategy 96: Target Realtors 182
Strategy 97: Increase business from Realtor referrals 185
Strategy 98: Add services without adding work 186
Strategy 99: Speed up the slow season 188

In Closing 192

Appendix A

Introduction

Five Reasons Why Marketing Fails

Everybody knows that marketing is necessary. It's the thing that generates interest, which in turn generates leads—and leads are what we need to make sales.

Marketing gets your name out, gets people thinking about you, and makes you the one they call when they need services like yours. Yet, as important as marketing is to growth, it is probably the most misunderstood and under-managed part of many businesses. Because of this, marketing fails more often than it succeeds.

It doesn't need to be this way. Marketing really is an essential part of growing your business, and if done correctly, it will generate plenty of leads and sales for you. This book is about mastering and managing marketing so that it does just that.

Before we start, though, let's look at why marketing fails for so many of us.

At the root of it all, there are five basic reasons why businesses don't get traction with their marketing:

i. No plan.
ii. No consistency.
iii. No completion.
iv. Procrastination.
v. Doing nothing.

Consider these more closely.

i. **No plan.** Success *never* happens by accident. Not once. If you keep doing what you've always done, you'll keep getting the results that you've always gotten. You've got to plan. If you don't have a plan, any road will look right, but you'll never achieve success. You must plan success. If you don't plan to succeed, you're certainly planning to fail. Plan how much you want to make and what strategies you are going to use to make that much. Planning isn't a big secret; it just takes time and commitment. Some people say they don't want to plan because they might change their minds. That's absurd. You can always alter your plan. Make your goals higher or lower. Pick a completely different goal. But if you don't have a plan, you'll never get anywhere. It's very important that you plan to succeed.

ii. **No consistency.** One of the reasons the market strategies in this book work so well is that they are systems. You need to do every part of the system to get it to run correctly. People are shocked when they just do the first step, and it doesn't work as well as they want it to. Well, would you be surprised if you put a tape in your VCR and nothing happened? Of course not—you know you have to plug it in, hook it up to the TV, put the TV on the correct channel, and then press "play." Then it plays. Not before. Well, it's the same with any system, including a marketing system. There are several parts that make the system work. And they do work—you just have to work with them. So you've got to be consistent.

iii. **No completion.** This is another big reason people fail. They get all excited about marketing strategy, and start a whole bunch of initiatives at once. They never give enough time to each one. They do all of them halfway, then wonder why it's not working. If you have too many things going at once, none of them will be profitable. Stick to five things to start with. Concentrate on one at a time. Get that one working, and then start another. Once you have all five of those things going, then pick another five. Don't try to do too much at once.

iv. **Procrastination.** Putting things off is a common reason marketing fails. "I'll get around to it tomorrow" has destroyed more businesses than you can imagine. Avoid making excuses like, "I don't have these tree or landscape evaluation forms made up, so I can't send out a letter," or "I don't know which neighborhoods are good, so I'll just wait," or "I don't know how to do this exactly right." So what if everything isn't perfect? It's much more important to do *something* than to wait for everything to be perfect—that won't happen. Do your best, give it a shot, then learn and improve. Procrastination is deadly. Don't wait—do it today. Do it right now. Pick out five actions, start on one, and get them going. Do not procrastinate.

v. **Doing nothing.** This is the number-one reason why marketing fails: The business owner or manager doesn't do anything—this is the killer. How can anyone possibly succeed if they don't do anything? They can't. So why do so many people do nothing?

I think it's because they're afraid to fail. They think if they try something, they're going to fail. Most people are afraid of failure. The thing is, everyone fails. I failed many, many times before I learned these marketing strategies. Even now, when I try something new, sometimes it fails. It doesn't bother me. Most of what I do succeeds—I definitely make a lot of money from the successes, but I learn more from the failures. There's nothing to be afraid of. If I never failed, I would never have succeeded: It's that simple. Don't be a victim of not doing anything. Do something. The main thing is to do something, because doing nothing, you certainly will not be successful.

This book is about eliminating these five root causes of failure and giving you the tools to get your marketing up, running, and growing your business. The ninety-nine strategies I've covered are based on my own experience and success in the tree care business, and I know they work.

If you need help, go to my Web site, *www.treecaresuccess.com,* and you should find plenty of help. Or shoot me a question, and I'll be glad to help you out.

John P. Davis
Marketing Coach to the Tree and Landscape Industry
RENEGADE Marketing Systems
817-222-9494
Boyd, Texas, 76117 USA

Section 1: First Things First

Marketing fundamentals of growing a successful business

Marketing success depends on more than just the mechanics. There is an intangible side to marketing that needs planning, preparation, and ongoing education. And because marketing needs be happening throughout your whole company, success also relies on your own abilities as a leader and manager. Therefore, it is really important to talk about the fundamentals that make your marketing work.

This section is divided into four parts:

1. Know where you are—and where you are going.
2. Be a marketing expert.
3. Be a great manager.
4. Be a leader.

Every strategy listed in this section will set you up to win at marketing, now and in the future.

Know where you are—and
where you are going

Strategy 1:
Have a marketing plan

The most important thing about marketing is to have a marketing plan. Most tree or landscape businesses fail because they do not have a plan or goal.

You should have a detailed marketing plan of what you want to accomplish and how you are going to accomplish it. Do not be vague about it. Do not state things such as "I want to make more money than I can ever spend," or "I want to be rich," or "I want to make $10,000 a month." These are not plans. They are too vague, and they simply will not help you get there. Be specific.

As you go through this book, pick at least five items to start with and write them down. Write down how much you are going to make on each idea this week and this month. Then do a three-month plan and a six-month plan. Once you start using the first five ideas, and then add another five, then another.

Soon, you should be using almost all of the money-making marketing strategies in this book. I say "most" because there might be one or two that are just not for you. That's okay. Use the ones that you are the most excited about to begin, and then branch out. Your plan should include many goals.

Your plan does not need to be put into a computer. It can be handwritten on paper. Do whatever works best for you and will allow you to keep track.

The important part is that you do a plan every single week and keep on top of things. Here at our business, we have a weekly meeting of all of our salespeople and staff. It lasts two hours, from 11:00 am to 1:00 pm. We meet to review our numbers. We meet to review any complaints. It gives us a time each week to review what happened in the previous week, what is happening with each salesperson, and any conflicts that may exist between office staff and salespeople.

It keeps things running, but also keeps you abreast of where you have been and where you are headed. That little strategy will certainly increase your numbers. So it is a good thing to get started pretty quickly.

Strategy 2:
Put numbers into the plan

Try to put your money goal in net to you, not gross. Gross is what you are used to thinking in, but net is obviously more important. If you run $500,000 in gross, it sounds impressive. But if you only net $35,000, it's not very impressive compared to gross.

First, examine your current numbers. Most tree or landscape owners or managers do not know how many clients they get a month. That is a deadly sin. You must know how you are doing currently. You should know how many new clients you get each month, how much you make from each client, and how much it costs you to acquire a new client.

Here is an example: Joe is a fictitious tree or landscape business owner. He has been in business for two years. He gets most his clients from low-balling his prices, and a few here and there from his Yellow Pages ad. He grosses $25,000 a month. His average job is $500; therefore, he does approximately twelve jobs a week. His net is 50 percent of gross, or a little more than $3,000 a week.

Now Joe wants to double his net income in two months, triple in four months, and I do not blame him. Consider that Joe does not know any of our marketing secrets; he will have to get twice as many jobs to double his business. His goal then would be twenty-four jobs a week. He currently gets eight to nine jobs from his low-ball, low-cost advertising, and two from his Yellow Pages ads. But he gets eighteen calls a week from his low-ball ads and five from his Yellow Pages ads. So he currently closes 50 percent of his prospects. If he does not learn any of my methods to improve his 50-percent closing ratio, then he will have to get forty-eight prospects to do twenty-four jobs. Here is his plan to get forty-eight prospects: fifteen consumer messages, five Yellow Pages leads, five network newsletters, nineteen prospecting newsletters, and three from his referral program: that is fifty-one prospects. Well, that is three more than his goal.

You should have a weekly plan. Schedule fifteen minutes out of one day to make up your weekly plan, and see how you did the last week. Schedule this time and keep to it. Do not make any appointments during this time. Keep it strictly for planning. If you do only this and nothing else I've provided here, you could easily double your income in twelve months.

Now, let me say it again: Plan weekly, scheduling maybe fifteen or thirty minutes out of one day to make up your weekly plan, and then check and see how you did last week. Schedule this time and keep to it. And, yes, you can very easily double your income in twelve months just by doing this and knowing where you have been and where you are headed.

Of course, Joe did not know any of our secrets to double the profit of all his jobs. If he did both—double his profit on each job and double the amount of jobs—he would quadruple his business in less than two months.

Your weekly plan should include the following:

1. A goal for the total net income.
2. A goal for the number of new clients.
3. A goal for the number of repeat clients.
4. A goal for the number of referrals.

You should have an average net income from each client. You should know the number of prospects you will have to generate to reach your goal. You need to know that number. You should also have a detailed plan to generate the number of prospects you need.

Why do it alone? Go to www.*treecaresuccess.com* and sign up for my "Millionaire Maker" Inner Circle Program.

Strategy 3:
Develop your Unique Selling Proposition

Your unique selling proposition (USP) is a precise statement of why your company is special. It should answer the prospect's question: Why should I do business with you versus any or all of your competitors? And you can expand on it: Why should I do business with you versus any or all of your competitors—or doing it myself? Don't worry if you cannot answer that question now. I will go over how to formulate your unique selling proposition.

First, I want to tell you how powerful a USP can be.

There was a college student who had to pay his way through college somehow. So he and his brother decided to open up a pizza place. Brother number one would run the place during the day and go to school at night, while brother number two would go to school during the day and run the place at night.

After a few months, they were losing more money than they were making, and brother number two wanted to get out, in exchange for an old beat up Volkswagen Rabbit.

Now brother number one owned the entire business. Not long after, brother number one developed a USP and turned his company into a multi-billion-dollar company within a very short time. This was his USP:

Fresh, hot pizza delivered in thirty minutes or less, guaranteed.

Of course, that is Domino's and that is how Tom's fortune was made. Now, they don't even guarantee the thirty-minute delivery, but that is irrelevant. They are so huge now and everyone knows them that it is not hurting them. But the USP made them big; it made the difference.

The important point is that a USP is not complicated, it is simple. It does not promise all things to all people. It never mentions the homemade sauce from the old country or even good taste like Mama makes. What it did was expand on an opportunity gap in the pizza-delivery business. No one was quick. It used to take at least an hour or longer. And it addressed another concern: People hate cold pizza.

If you see an opportunity gap in your area, go for it. One of the biggest opportunity gaps is giving a small time window. Most people hate to wait around all day or even four hours. They are annoyed, but no one has offered them a different alternative. You can dominate your market if you hit an opportunity gap.

I have a landscape mentor in Ohio, Marty Grunder of the Winners Circle and Grunder's Landscape. He began to set up his appointments at 9:57, 10:57, and 11:57, and so on. This made him stand out in his market. He would be standing at the door at 9:56 or 10:56, waiting for the homeowner to come out once he rang the doorbell at that precise time. You may say, "Well, that sounds a little silly," but what it did was set him apart in his marketplace. It got him talked about and an article in the paper about him for doing that one simple thing. So he drove in a lot of business.

Most tree-care companies—and we all know this—just say, "I will be out there sometime today," or they may say, "We'll be there sometime this week." That is a very bad thing to do.

You need to begin to be more precise. I know you have to give a window, but what you should try to do is no more than a two-hour window, if at all possible. Don't keep your clients waiting all day. It just creates irritated people.

How do you decide on your USP? You should think this over for a while. Do not rush it. Your USP is very important. You should mention it in all of your marketing materials, even on your vehicles. This turns your company vehicles and equipment into functional marketing tools. Most vehicle signs do not say a thing. No one is generally interested in the name of your company. They want to know why they should do business with you. Plaster your USP on every marketing piece.

Talk to your clients. See what they really like about you, why they chose you, what else they want from you, what they hate most. This is a very important question to ask: What do they hate most about doing business with you (or other tree-care firms)? That will get you a wealth of information.

Analyze all these answers from many different clients. Out of all of that, decide which points are most important. Then narrow your USP down to one to three sentences. One long sentence is better, but you can go up to three. Start using it. Use it in all your marketing materials, and also in your everyday life. When you meet someone new, they almost always ask, "What do you do?" When they ask that, you start selling.

Your USP should convey one or two major benefits that create interest. For example, my USP for our tree-care firm is this: "The Most Thorough Tree Care **_EVER_**. . .or it's FREE!" We will go over strong guarantees later.

I use this USP in public-speaking engagements, at workshops, even on the street. People then ask only one question: "Really? How do you do that?" That is what you want your prospects to do when you tell them.

So, create your USP and start using it. It is a very important thing.

Strategy 4:
Set your pricing standards

Do you know the difference between price and value? Price is what you pay. Value is what you get. Everyone wants a good value. They do not want a low price if they get crummy service. They want value. Give them value and charge them for it.

You can charge anything you want, as long as you convince people you are worth it. That is not hard to do.

But, **_if you live by price, you will die by price_**.

What I mean by this is that if you are the cheapest in town, you will probably go out of business.

Cheapest is terrifying to me. I would never want to be the cheapest. I would much rather do three jobs and make $1,000 than ten jobs and make the same amount for the same work. Quality, not quantity.

There are a few big national stores that deliver low prices by having a huge turnover. You and I are not huge. You and I cannot make up in quantity. It is just too much work trimming trees, and there are only so many hours in a day.

Cheap prices lead to inferior work. Inferior work leads to unhappy clients. Unhappy clients lead to no repeat business and no referrals. It is only a matter of time before the cheapest company goes out of business. Of course, there will always be another company to replace the one that went out of business, but just do not let that be you.

I have one of the most expensive tree companies in the area, but I still get tons of clients because I convince them that they are getting a great value, **_and they are_**.

Note that I say, "the most expensive tree or landscape company in the area," and it is, if you look at pricing per hour. It is not expensive to the client when you begin to see what they get.

Think of how much more you do than your competitors.

When you put this marketing program into force, this is what you can say. You may already. You offer a solid, risk-free guarantee. You live up to your promises. You do great work. You strive for quality. You educate your clients. You do more for them than they ever think they paid for. You are superior, so you should get paid for it. If you are convinced you are worth it, your clients will be too.

Don't focus on competing on price; focus on value. Set your pricing standards based on the value you give to your clients, and then make sure to educate and remind them about this value.

Be a marketing expert

Strategy 5:
Learn everything for yourself

Getting this book was the best thing you ever did for your business. But you have to learn it all for yourself.

You cannot trust Yellow Pages reps or any advertising reps. You cannot even trust advertising agencies. At one time, I listened to all of them. I tried everything. The only thing I learned was that very few of them have a clue about how to get new clients. I hired an ad agency. That was the biggest mistake of my life. I even decided to hire an image-building advertising agency. I thought that was going to be the end of my troubles. I couldn't really afford it, but I thought I would get a ton of business. The advertising agency was great, great at making pretty-looking ads and building my image. After a while, I was losing so much money, I realized advertising agencies don't have an idea about how to actually get new clients.

I learned a very important lesson: If an ad doesn't work once, it won't work the second or third time either. I fell for the old saying, "If you just run it again, this time people will respond."

The theory behind it is that people need to see ads more than just once before they respond. There is some minor truth in this; however, if an ad loses money the first time, it is not suddenly going to make a ton of money the second or third time. Finally, I started using emotional direct-response marketing, and I succeeded.

Learn for yourself. Don't trust any of those image-building types. When you try something new, track your numbers carefully so you know whether it is working or not. You have to do that.

Strategy 6:
Constantly learn

People forget. You forget. I forget. It is a fact of life. So how can we overcome this? The trick is space-repetitive learning. That is, to go over things many times with a span of time in between.

Have you ever listened or watched something for the second time and realized you missed a major point the first time? You may even notice that the way I go through these strategies is to hit one item, then go through other items, and then refer back to the first, and to keep doing that. We are coming back with a little different spin. It is a better learning process than hitting all points on one subject and then moving to another one.

So, back to learning marketing. To get the most out of this powerful book, you are going to have to read it five to seven times; not at once, but over a period of twelve months. Each time you read it, you will get more out of it. You'll learn more and more money-making strategies. Repetition is the key to learning.

Learn all you can about marketing. Get books, tapes, letters, videos, everything you can get your hands on—you are in the marketing business. We all are. Whether we own a parts store or a tree or landscape business, it does not matter. The truth is that we all need new clients. So whether we like it or not, we are all in the marketing business.

Once you know great marketing strategies that make gobs of money, marketing becomes great fun. But don't stop with this book. Keep learning more and more about marketing, unless, of course, you do not want to make any more money—or have any more time off!

Strategy 7:
Attend industry meetings

You'll see many benefits from associations you belong to. Granted, sometimes they're boring, but you can meet some really interesting tree and landscape people. New and exciting methods are two of the benefits you get from other tree or landscape people you meet at these meetings.

Learn new methods to try. Learn new and better ways to use less labor and materials. You can also receive new ideas for different products and services to offer your clients. Granted, some of these tree and landscape people aren't willing to share any of their ideas, and some don't have any worthwhile ideas to share, but some do. Those are the ones you want to form relationships with.

Tree care and landscape associations keep you on top of things. You go back more inspired than before. You learn a lot, and teach a lot. I strongly suggest trying one out. If you haven't been to them, in the tree care industry, it's the Tree Care Industry Association (TCIA), the TCIA Expo, the International Society of Arboriculture, meetings; in landscape, it's American Landscape Contractors Association, and different associations that you need to be at. You'll find a lot of new strategies and a lot of new things. More importantly, you'll find things that don't work and can save yourself a lot of money by not falling into the same traps. You'll avoid a lot of potholes.

Strategy 8:
Read trade journals

To stay motivated and interested, you have to keep up and keep learning new things about your business—new marketing strategies, new techniques, new equipment, new products, etc. A good source of information is trade journals. They're an easy way to stay on the cutting edge of industry.

Always keep learning and improving. This is what makes tree or landscape fun; it's what makes landscaping fun. Once you stop learning, you start to stagnate. You just sit there. Pretty soon, that booming business isn't booming anymore. Don't let this happen.

The trade journals are a great source to see what others are doing. To see what new materials and new equipment are out there to make your job easier. Trade journals are an easy and very inexpensive way to keep up with the times in your particular industry. So, read the trade journals and be on the mailing lists of all of them.

Strategy 9:
Learn by example

Just like anything else that you learn, you learn from good examples.

For instance, you have a wealth of information that you probably throw away every day. You think of it as junk mail, but this "junk" mail can give you a wealth of knowledge. Do not underestimate it. More money is spent on direct-mail advertising than any other media. That's right. More businesses spend money on direct mail than TV advertising. Why? Because it works and you don't have to spend a fortune to find out if your piece works or not. In other media, you have to spend a lot of money just to find out if it works. That is another reason why direct mail is so great.

Stop throwing away that junk mail and start reading it. Separate your junk mail into two piles: one for what you think is good and one for what you think is bad. Try rewriting the bad ones to get some practice. Think of things that can improve the good ones. Pretty soon, you are going to become a marketing maniac.

Strategy 10:
"Steal" marketing ideas

I don't mean *literally* steal or even plagiarize.

I mean *learn from others*. Use ideas that are working for others. There isn't any reason why they won't work for you too. You can test ideas and examples inexpensively.

So you test, test, test!

For many years when I went to TCI expos, trade shows, and meetings, one of my main goals was to get answers to a list of questions. I would try to single out someone who appeared to be successful, and I would ask questions and get different ideas about marketing. I spent most of my time on the tradeshow floor, and not a lot of my time at the seminars. I would talk to the exhibitors and other owners and managers. I always came home with a wealth of information that didn't cost me a dime.

I also got on different tree care companies' newsletter lists. It was a great opportunity to see what others were doing (both in my area and elsewhere), and gave me great ideas to try in my own company.

Don't limit yourself to "stealing" ideas just from tree or landscape companies. Model good ideas from other successful businesses. Most ideas can be applied in some way to your business.

For example, do you think the fast-food industry invented the drive-through window? No, they stole the idea from banks (or, they creatively stole it).

You can imagine how this happened. One day, a guy from McDonald's was sitting in his car at the bank drive-through, and it occurred to him. He said, "I am not sure how the drinks will fit...but otherwise it is perfect." And of course, the fast-food industry was changed forever.

So you can see, you get great ideas in any kind of business. Keep your eyes peeled and always think, "How can I apply this to my business?"

I keep a swipe file. It is basically a wealth of stuff that I get in my mailbox. Look at the direct mail that you keep getting in the mail. If you keep getting it, there is a reason. It is simply because they are successful.

So, study these. Look at the ideas. Look at how they do it. Look at the sequence of mailings that is used. Then ask, "How can I adapt this to build my business?" You are now on the road to being a professional copywriter and marketer without spending hundreds of thousands of dollars.

You are looking at material that costs thousands of dollars and sometimes millions to be produced by different mega-marketing companies.

Change it over to your particular landscaping business, tree business, or any business, and you are way ahead of the game.

Be a great manager

Strategy 11:
Do something

Sounds simple, right? Well, let's talk about it. Remember, the number-one reason people fail in marketing is because they never do it. They learn all these money-making marketing strategies and they do not use them.

It is better to do something that isn't quite perfect than not to do anything at all. Don't worry if you do not have every little thing you need.

For instance, if you do a letter giving away a "Tree Hazard Evaluation," don't worry if you get overwhelmed; test the method. If you get a huge response, just tell your clients that you are overwhelmed with the response and you are currently a little behind, but go ahead and get them on your schedule. This is much, much better than doing nothing at all.

Once you try something, then you have a place to go from there. Even if your method did not work as well as you would like, you will be able to improve it and get more response. Stop worrying about all the little details—just *begin*. Take the first step, start doing it. You will be very glad you did.

Strategy 12:
Be consistent

On again, off again. It is a bad habit, and a very costly one for your business. If you truly want to succeed and net $125,000 or more per year, you are going to have to be consistent.

Let's say there is a competitor who has okay market strategies, okay letters, and okay bids. He does not have exceptional marketing strategy or ads, but he consistently makes $100,000 or more a year.

How?

He is consistent with his market strategies and his follow-up. He could be better. A lot better. But consistency is extremely important.

Another company with sensational ads and sensational letters barely makes $45,000 a year. Why? Simply because of inconsistency. He does not track his results; the owner does not really know what is working and what isn't.

A lot of people will tell you things are truly working for them, and then when you analyze the numbers, you find out they are not. The same is true for things people don't think are working.

Unless you know your numbers, you don't know what is working and what is not.

Almost every time I talk to business owners or salespeople, they tell me how they are too busy to send thank-you notes.

With this type of response, you realize you won't be busy in a few months.

With this lack of service, you are more than likely guaranteed the same old story.

"It is dead. I don't have any customers."

Why did this happen? It is quite simple: Lack of consistency. You must be consistent in everything you do concerning marketing.

Strategy 13:
Stay on top of things

You can easily stay on top of things if you schedule specific times each week to see how you are doing and make new goals. Monday morning between 8:00 and 8:30 works very well for me. Keep this meeting. Do not schedule appointments or anything else during this time. Keep this appointment with yourself every week.

Look over your marketing goals for last week. How did you do? If you did not do as well as you wanted to, then change some things so you will do better next week. If you did better than you had expected, then keep on doing what you are doing. It is very important to keep track of how you are doing. Know your numbers.

During this time, you should decide what new strategies you are going to implement over the next week. If you are consistent, you will stay on top of these things.

Strategy 14:
Get employees involved

You know how it works: You do everything right, only to have it spoiled by indifferent employees. So you need to motivate them to give great service by offering some kind of reward.

Here is a very cheap way to drastically increase referrals, get repeat business, and cut way back on your complaints and redos. All of this for very little expense.

Here is how it works at my company. Every crew chips in and buys postage for postcards.

We furnish them with postcards with our company return address printed on the cards.

After each job, they write a small note on the card, asking the client to comment on the job and the employees on the job. They then give the card to the client or they leave it on their door.

For every card mailed back with rave reviews or very good comments, each employee on that job gets five dollars.

This is a very good way to get testimonials and a very good way to see what clients think about your employees.

But another great thing it does is show your clients that you are thinking about *them*. It shows them that you want to do a great job for them.

You are going to see that clients love to do things for employees.

Now, it is very important that the client *mails* the card in. Do not allow employees to have the client fill it out on the spot. This puts undue pressure on the client. If they think an employee is going to get some benefit out of it, they will certainly do it. You will also get some rave reviews, and also find out if a job was not done well.

On the employee side, they know they are leaving that card, so it is hard for them to do a bad job. They know that you are going to find out about their work in the mail. You might think that an employee just wouldn't leave a card, but in most cases, there is peer pressure on the crew not to allow that to happen. We get hundreds and hundreds of cards every year. It is a very effective thing that you certainly want to do.

Strategy 15:
Keep employees informed and educated

Employees can be a wonderful source of referrals. In order for a business to be extremely successful, the employees have to believe in it too. Once you educate your employees on why you deliver such a great service, you will be surprised at the rewards. This is what will happen:

1. Your employees will start selling a lot more. If, for example, they don't know why fertilization is necessary or how it helps, then they won't sell it. But if you educate your employees, they will know and be much more likely to try to sell it.

2. Your employees can be a wealth of referrals. If they don't think your company is exceptional, they won't refer anyone. But if you taught them why and they truly believe it, they will tell lots and lots of people.

3. An educated employee is much better suited to help and answer questions from a client. Clients get very annoyed when employees don't know anything.

Educate your employees on a regular basis. Get them excited about working for such a wonderful company. Education and motivation are the keys to super-great employees. Go over why fertilization works. Go over why trees need to be pruned. Go over why you think things are done. If you educate them, then they are going to be able to answer these questions from the client and make you look a whole lot better in the marketplace. Make sure they know why they do what they do.

Strategy 16:
Motivate employees

Here is one way to motivate employees, a way to get them to work hard: Host weekly and monthly contests. You can have the same contest every week and then have others that change.

For instance, you can have a contest for the foreman or salesperson that gets the most referrals. This is a great one. You can give the winner a bonus of $25 or $50. This makes your arborists compete against each other. No longer will they forget to ask for referrals. No more days of complaining about it—they'll be happy to do it.

You also should have a contest where anyone can win—offer twenty dollars to everyone who gets at least three referrals in a week, or ten referrals in a week, or five referrals in a week.

You can also have employee-of-the-month awards based on referrals, competence, and hard work. You can have a competition for the greatest number of outside jobs. An outside job is a job the employee gets himself—his friends, relatives, and associates.

Make the reward big enough to motivate your employees. Even if it's $200, if you get your employees to get ten jobs, that didn't cost you any advertising money. You did very well.

Put all of these contests up on the bulletin board, and track everyone's results on the board daily (if it's a weekly contest) or weekly (if it's a monthly contest). It's natural for people to be competitive and motivated by money. Take advantage of this, and it will really get your people to be working on it.

Strategy 17:
Get rid of "bad apple" customers

Clients who are problems all the time should be fired. That's right—fire your bad clients. What do I mean? Fire bad clients when I keep preaching about client service and client satisfaction?

You must look at it this way:

Excellent client service *is* crucial—crucial to those who are *good* clients. If a client is not satisfied with anything and always complains, that person isn't worth the headaches, no matter how much business they give you.

Long ago, I decided I wouldn't give superior service to the bad apples. Bad apples can ruin the whole lot—and you. They aren't worth it.

If you feel you've done more than what is expected, and have done a great job, and someone keeps complaining, just fire them. Even give them their money back, just to get rid of them. If you don't, these bad apples have very big mouths. Even though they're being completely unreasonable, others won't perceive it that way. So gladly give them their money back and get rid of them.

Life is too short; there are too many good people out there to waste your time on the bad apples.

Strategy 18:
Work on your business, not in your business

What in the world does this mean?

"Working *in* your business" means going out and doing actual technical work: Being a salesperson, scheduling jobs, managing employees—any of those things are working *in* your business.

"Working *on* your business" is planning what service you want to expand into, what new niche do you want to target, how many new trucks will you expand into? It's just marketing and testing your market, etc.

Do you get the difference?

You probably work *in* your business now—that's okay. But you also need to work *on* your business. If you don't, no one else will. You need to plan to be successful. As you grow and get bigger, you should work less and less in your business. You can hire others to do that. You can't hire anyone to work on your business. You have to do that.

This is a very powerful strategy, getting outside your business and beginning to work on it as a separate entity. This strategy is what Walt Disney used to create the huge Disney empire—Disney World, Disneyland, and all the Disney characters, Disney movies, etc. Disney is one of the most successful companies in America. One of the reasons for this is that people at the top work *on* the business, they don't work *in* the business.

This same strategy will work for you, too. Work less and less in your business, and more and more on your business, and you'll see great results.

Need systems for your business? Go to www.treecaresuccess.com and sign up for membership in my "Millionaire Maker" Inner Circle Program.

Be a leader

Strategy 19:
Use time in your vehicle to keep learning

How much time do you spend in your vehicle every day? Probably at least an hour. Maybe up to three hours or more if you are a salesperson.

And what do you normally do when you drive? You listen to music, think, different things, but probably nothing very productive. What I am going to ask you to do is stop wasting time in your car and start your own private mobile college, learning more about marketing and other business matters.

There are many marketing programs on tapes and CDs. You can begin to turn your unproductive time into super-productive learning time. This works very well. I usually listen to educational tapes or other business-related tapes when I am driving around in my vehicle.

So, giving up listening to music is a small price to pay to learn valuable information that you can make millions with. And if you are at a loss as to what tapes are available or what tapes really have good information, just give me a call and I will certainly point you in the right direction.

Also, having said that, I not only recommend my material at *www.treecaresuccess.com,* but also marketing guru Dan Kennedy's material, which can be obtained at this same site. I have a lot of sales and marketing programs that I can get to you very reasonably for use in your vehicle and for other study time that will make a tremendous difference in your business.

So, make a university out of your car. Use time that you do not usually use productively—this will certainly get you ahead of the game.

Strategy 20:
Be professional

This is something that really needs to be preached more in our industry. We see it all the time. What do I mean by being professional? Here are some examples:

- Have a clean truck. Even an older truck can be clean.
- Have everyone in uniforms—same-color pants with a clean logo T-shirt is fine. We use a uniform company. We have uniform shirts, and everyone wears the same color pants.
- Everyone should be well-groomed. No two-day stubble or straggly hair. Check your people when they arrive in the morning. Have a razor available; whatever it takes. Make sure they look neat. Beards are fine, moustaches are fine, and goatees are fine, as long as they are neat. Make sure they look how you want the people to see you, because remember, they *are* you.

The public is skeptical about tree or landscape companies. The reason is because there are a lot of so-called tree or landscape companies out there that rip people off. We must overcompensate for their bad reputation. We just have to do it. Granted, this is unfair, but that's the way it is.

I see many companies go to homes with dirty trucks. I have seen crews who did not have uniforms on at all. They have on dirty jeans, old ripped T-shirts, their hair is a mess, they haven't shaved in about a week, and sometimes they have no shirts on.

You must look clean, neat, and organized. This earns people's trust and respect. No one wants someone looking like that to come to their house for anything. Clean trucks are important. I get quite a few calls from people who saw one of our trucks in their neighborhood and needed our service. Do you think they would call if the truck had been dirty? Absolutely not. I am not saying you have to have a brand-new BMW truck, but I am saying your company needs to look good.

Our trucks are traveling billboards. I am not saying you need to buy new trucks all the time, but keep what you have clean.

Throw a new paint job on them in the winter in your slow time. Paint does not cost that much. Keep a magnetic logo sign and use it as a traveling billboard. We make thousands of dollars a year off of the signs that are on our trucks. We have them designed and built so we can put billboard-type signs on the side of them. People know that we are in the area.

It makes a big difference to make sure your people are projecting the image that you want. It does absolutely no good for you to go out and meet a prospective client in your nice truck, looking and sounding fine and sharp, only to be followed by your messy crew. The client will wonder, is this the same company? Are these the same people I hired? And it puts a bad taste in their mouth.

So you really need to keep on top of that.

Strategy 21:
Model top-notch ethics

You can't possibly build a big, strong company if you're not ethical.

It's just that simple.

It's business suicide to be unethical. Most businesses that are unethical are so because they think it saves them money. This is absolutely ridiculous; it's insane. Maybe in the short run, it saves them money, but in the long run, it's a big mistake. It's fatal. Why?

An unhappy client will tell the world how you are unfair and unethical. They'll gripe to everyone they know—even the people they don't know. A few clients who are unhappy can easily destroy your business.

So make them happy!

If they're truly jerks, you don't want to do business with them. Give them their money back. I don't care if you've already done the work—believe me; it's much cheaper to give them their money back than to let them tell the world how you ripped them off.

Live up to your promises. So many businesses just don't live up to their promises. It's sad, and very bad for business. Don't make promises you can't keep. For the most part, a client isn't going to decide if he or she is going to do business with you based on one promise. Never promise the things you can't do.

If you can't arrive at the client's house within a half-hour window, then don't promise that. Or promise if you don't, she'll get $20 off of her bill, but don't flat-out promise something you can't deliver, or something you're not positive you can deliver.

Explain why you can't deliver something a client would like.

Educating your client is a million times better than breaking a promise. Being ethical won't just help you sleep better at night; it just makes good business sense.

Strategy 22:
Hold yourself accountable

No excuses. No lies. You have to hold yourself accountable for everything, the good and the bad.

Luck? That is nonsense.

A marketing acquaintance of mine in the landscape business puts it this way: "The harder I work, the luckier I get." Luck? Nonsense again. Everything that happens in your business is the result of your work—or lack thereof. *Everything.*

Stop blaming the economy or the season or whatever. The economy is good or bad, right between your ears.

If you need more help, go to *www.treecaresuccess.com* or call my office and check out all of our tools for the tree and landscape industry. You can have all the tools you need to be hugely successful.

Start counting on yourself. Make plans and stick to them. You will be the reason your company succeeds or fails.

Strategy 23:
Remove mental garbage

Most of us have lots of mental garbage. "Mental garbage" describes ideas and thoughts that you and I have been saying since we were born. Mental garbage means thought and ideas that are wrong, dead wrong, but we've heard them over and over until we believe them. Thoughts such as:

1. **If you work hard, you will succeed.** This is complete garbage. Do you remember that smart kid in school who never studied but always received A's? He didn't work hard. Then there's that kid who studied all the time and only received Bs. Now, *he* worked hard. Working hard does not ensure success.

   Before I started using these strategies, when I was broke, I worked hard. Much, much harder than I work now. I didn't know what to do, so I worked on a lot of things that didn't get us any clients. Now that I know these powerful strategies, I don't have to work hard; I work smarter, not harder.

2. **If you're good at what you do, you'll have plenty of clients.** Yeah, right. This is bogus. I used to do just as good a job as I do now. But I had very little business. I didn't know what to do to get repeat business or referrals or new clients. I was good, but nobody beat a path to my door.

3. **Your sales letters have to be done by a professional.** This is ridiculous. When you use professional letters, you usually won't get any new clients. Why? Because they're boring. But when you use creative, down-to-earth, easy-to-understand language in your letters, your newsletters, and your marketing, you'll get a lot more response.

To be successful, you have to get rid of this mental garbage. All it's doing is keeping you from success. Once you unload it, you'll be free to make as much money as you want, get as many clients as you want.

Get rid of mental garbage—all the preconceived notions—and you'll be way ahead of the game.

Strategy 24:
Keep yourself motivated

When you're bored and depressed, you can't possibly get new clients. They see your attitude and simply don't want to do business with you.

You first have to get your excitement and motivation back; then you'll get clients. Start using the new strategies in this book, ones you've never used before. Once you start to get over your depression, your slump will be history.

Remember, success breeds success. It's true. If you want to be successful, start hanging around with successful people. Once you get out of your slump, keep doing new things. Keep learning and keep up your excitement.

You control whether or not you go into another slump—it's totally up to you.

Strategy 25:
Stay in tune with your clients, staff, and service

As business owners and entrepreneurs, we delegate the daily activities necessary to operate our businesses, but there is one activity that we can't delegate: our own personal responsibility to grow the business.

As entrepreneurs, many of us become comfortably complacent, never attempting to exploit and enjoy the true potential within our businesses. What contributes to the continuance of this problem is the fact that nobody is holding us accountable. Nobody is pushing us to get off our duffs and get busy developing our business to its true potential.

Many entrepreneurs suffer from mediocrity. They feel comfortable with the business in its present condition, its size, the income derived from it, the level of service it provides, etc. They choose to stay in the status quo, and they soon stagnate. The fact that you purchased this book proves that you are not this kind of individual. Congratulations!

Unfortunately, there's a little bit of that mediocrity in all of us. It's human nature to accept things the way they are; okay. So take the bull by the horns. Instead of the typical entrepreneurial mindset of looking at your business as a shrine, begin to look at it with the mindset of a wrecking ball. Listen to clients and employees. Seek change. Seek growth.

Section 2: How to Make Big Things Happen

Getting the tools, attitudes, and strategies right to bring in lots of business

We have talked fundamentals. Now it's time to talk about the tools and techniques that make up your marketing plan and program, as well as concepts and approaches that will be part of your activities.

This section is divided into four parts:

1. Marketing communications
2. Customer service
3. Making new sales
4. Making more sales

It is full of tried, tested, and proven strategies and ideas that will build your business in leaps and bounds.

Why do it alone? Go to www.*treecaresuccess.com* and sign up for membership in my "Millionaire Maker" Inner Circle Program.

Marketing communications

Strategy 26:
Write copy that sells

Writing good ads and sales letters isn't really that complicated.

First of all, forget everything that your high school English teacher taught you. If you're like most people, you're taught to write boring, complete sentences. Maybe they were grammatically correct, but they sure didn't sell anything.

What you want to concentrate on is connecting with the reader—the reader of your letter or ad. Make readers feel like you know them. Write about what they're interested in. Write about what they want. If you don't know what they want—ask your clients.

They'll tell you.

After all, you want more clients like the ones you already have (the good ones, that is).

Your letters should be you on paper. So write like you talk. Don't worry about grammar. Don't worry about complete sentences. They'll mess you up. One-word sentences are great when used in the right spots. They really get the point across.

Really.

Remember when you had to read something for school? You opened the book and there were just pages and pages of solid text—long paragraphs, boring copy. Discouraging, wasn't it? You don't want your reader to be discouraged, or he or she won't read it. Just like you didn't in school. Don't make it more difficult than it is; just write.

Write short sentences and short paragraphs.

Use a headline and lots of subheads.

Remember, a headline is the main point of what you write. It's the ad for the ad, if you want to put it that way.

Compose the headline and subheads so that the reader can get the message just by reading those.

These things make your copy easier to read.

And the easier it is to read, the more people will read it.

If you really have a problem with this strategy, go back and reread, then read the next one.

Strategy 27:
Tape record yourself

If you think you can't write an emotional sales copy, begin by tape recording yourself.

When most people start writing emotional direct-response copy, they get a little overwhelmed. This is natural. You have to unlearn years and years of learning. At school, we are taught to write in this incredibly boring, grammatically correct way. Although it may have worked to please your teachers, it doesn't work in selling, and it certainly doesn't work in getting profits.

Most people do a pretty good job in selling their service face-to-face. You close many, many sales when you give a quote. You know what to say, and create a desire for your services. So instead of trying to write a letter from scratch, stick a voice-activated recorder in your pocket and record yourself in action. Do this several times so you get used to it; you'll forget that it's even there.

Now, write out exactly what you've recorded (or have it transcribed for you). Leave it all in one-word sentences if that's the way it comes out. Don't worry about grammar or all those other boring rules. They don't make one bit of difference, and in fact, can actually hurt you when you're selling.

A sales letter is selling in print.

It should represent your voice on paper.

By tape recording yourself, you'll make the whole process of writing much, much easier.

This is the best way to do it.

One thing: Remember to get permission from the people you are tape recording. Let them know what you are doing and that their names won't get used in your writing, unless they agree.

Strategy 28:
Use direct-response marketing

We actually call this "emotional direct-response marketing." What is a direct-response ad? It is an ad that contains all of the following:

1. A headline
2. Words that create interest in the service or product
3. Words that create desire in the prospect
4. A specific offer
5. A deadline or cutoff date.

Most advertising in magazines, newspapers, radio, or TV are not direct-response. That is institutional advertising. There is no way of accurately tracking responses.

Why? There is no specific offer.

Why do advertising agencies like institutional advertising?

Well, very simple: They cannot be held responsible for the results, since there's no certain tracking mechanism. When an ad campaign does not produce sales, they blame it on the economy, or they talk about "long-term investment" and tell you that you need to run ads that did not work over again, and suddenly, they will just start working.

And they keep sending those invoices to you, even though no sales show up.

Out of the two "excuses," the second is by far the worst. Advertising agencies are notorious for saying, "Well, the public just needs to see your ad more often, and you will start getting more sales."

Many people believe this, and then waste a lot of money.

And still do not get results.

That theory is simply flawed. If an ad does not work at all once, it is not suddenly going to start bringing in lots of money.

It does not work that way.

But there is a tiny bit of truth to it.

A very, very small percentage of your response will come from people who have seen the ad before. This is the frosting on the cake, and certainly not enough to substantiate wasting more money.

Advertising agencies are interested in being creative. Many think about winning awards more than about selling the goods they are advertising. Interestingly, many ads that have won top awards do not produce any substantial increase in sales.

Building name recognition through institutional advertising is only possible with a huge, huge advertising budget. There is a lot of waste in that type of advertising, but some really big companies can survive that waste. Businesses like McDonald's or Domino's. They can afford this massive waste.

Small and local businesses do not have that option.

You can't do that.

I can't afford to waste marketing dollars on an ad that does not pull in immediate sales.

Direct response is result-oriented. You know exactly how much money you made from jobs that come from each direct-response method.

Emotional direct-response marketing gives your prospects something they want and tells them exactly what to do to get it. It gives them compelling reasons to use it. It gets response, and response means dollars.

Here are some rules of emotional direct-response marketing:

1. Never do anything that you cannot directly track the results.
2. Never run an ad a second time that did not work the first time.
3. Never fall in love with your ad.

The last item is a common mistake for people first starting out with direct marketing.

Remember that an ad is only good if it gets results.

Do not fall in love with any ad until you have tested it and know that it pulls.

Become a student of direct marketing.

Learn everything you can about it. The more you learn about marketing, the more money you will make.

If you would like to know about other books and things that can teach you more about direct marketing, check out all the marketing tools at my Web site, *www.treecaresuccess.com.*

Strategy 29:
Master direct mail

Direct mail is one of the most powerful ways to market your company. This year, there will be $29 million spent on direct mail, and it goes up every year by millions. There would not be that much money spent on direct mail if it did not work. So why do most small and medium tree and landscape service companies think of direct mail as a waste?

They do not know how to use it. They have never had any instruction on how to use it. They send a flyer out. They send it to a bad list.

The list of people who you send your letter to is just as important as the letter itself. Most people overlook this.

I was told one company had written a sales letter. It was pretty good, not great, but pretty good. It was getting zero response. Not one, but zero, zilch, nada.

Who were these letters being sent to?

They did not know.

They had bought a Zip Code zone. So, finally, he went to look at the houses in the Zip Code he had purchased. Run-down, tiny houses with broken porches that had at least one plank of wood missing. Junk strewn across the front yards and in the driveways. At one house, there was a car on cement blocks with half the engine removed. Both the husband and wife were sitting on the front porch, wearing stained T-shirts, with matching beer cans in their hands.

Are these the type of people most likely to buy your services?

If they ever had their trees trimmed, which is highly doubtful, they would borrow a saw, get some beer, and call their buddies and try to do it themselves. These people were not good prospects. The list is very important.

To recap, here is why most tree or landscapes and landscape companies fail at direct mail.

1. No direct-mail expertise.
2. Bad sales letter.
3. Simply a bad list.

How to do successful direct mail:

1. Have an irresistible offer. The more enticing your offer, the better you will sell.
2. Attention getting headlines: One of the most important things is a headline. It is really an ad for your sales letter. It is what directs them to the rest of the letter.
3. Interest: Create interest. The first paragraph should emphasize the benefit to the reader. This gets the prospect interested enough to read the rest of the letter.
4. Desire: Make your prospect really want what you are offering.
5. Action: Again, you must have an irresistible offer.
6. Deadline: You must have a deadline. If you do not have an expiration date, you do not have a direct-response ad. You must have a deadline to have a direct-response letter and a reason to use your services at that time.

Strategy 30:
Use letters, not brochures

Fancy three-panel brochures are very expensive. And they don't work. Why?

They immediately yell out, "THIS IS A SALES MESSAGE!"

Once someone thinks you are trying to sell them something, they are much less receptive.

Have you ever seen the cartoon with General Patton? Patton is in the middle of a huge battle and a man comes up to him with a box full of guns. Patton says, "I don't have time for a salesman right now, I'm in the middle of a war."

You see, even if you have exactly what the prospect needs, if they think you are a salesman, it is going to be very difficult for you to get through to them. It is the same thing with your sales message. A brochure is immediately recognized as a sales message. It is fancy but boring.

With brochures, you cannot cheaply and easily change your message. Things can change quickly. Maybe you decide to offer or discontinue a particular service. You can't change your brochure, so you either have inaccurate information, or you have to spend a ton of money all over again to get it redone.

Another reason brochures don't work is that you cannot cheaply test them. You should always test, test, test. With brochures, you have to get a lot printed at once. If it doesn't work, you have a lot of wasted money.

Letters look and feel personal.

People think of letters as personal and brochures as sales.

Letters are inexpensive.

You get as few done at a time as you need.

Your money won't be tied up in inventory.

All of your marketing dollars will be out there working for you.

Letters are easily changed.

If something about your business changes, you can quickly, easily, and inexpensively change your sales message.

If your letter didn't work as well as you would like, you can easily improve it.

Strategy 31:
Use form letters and cards

Form letters or cards make follow-up a cinch. To be effective, you must have procedures (see Section 3 for more on that).

Many people claim they are good at follow-ups. When you inquire what procedures they have to follow up with, this is what I found out: They didn't have any.

They considered follow-up to be calling someone when they owed them money.

This is not a follow-up.

Anyone can do that, even a rank amateur.

Follow-up is a group of procedures that you do consistently. Remember, we talked earlier about consistency. Consistency is the key to making these marketing strategies work. You should have procedures for the following:

1. Thank-you letters and cards thanking someone for referring someone to you.
2. Reminders when they need their trees pruned or fertilized again, or additional landscaping.
3. New client kits.
4. Complaint response sheet.
5. Reminders of other services that you offer.
6. A well-written survey.

Form letters and cards make many of these strategies very easy, because many things you contact one client about will be the same thing you need to contact another client about. All you need to do is plug in your information into the areas, and you are set to go. When you need to use one, plug in the client's name and sign and mail. It is simply that easy, but you need to systemize how you do it and make sure it is done consistently.

Strategy 32:
Don't be boring!

Boring is a cardinal sin in marketing. I can't emphasize it enough. You get boring, they quit reading it. Longer copy only out pulls shorter copy if it is not boring.

How do you find out if your letters or cards or ads are boring or not?

Of course, you can mail out a couple hundred letters and cards and see what kind of response you get, but that could be very expensive, especially if it's boring.

When you're done with your letter, ad, or whatever, let ten people you know read your letter. If they say, "Yeah, that was good," go back to the drawing board. They're just being polite. When it's *really* good, they will start asking you more questions about how they can get what you offer.

If five people out of ten ask you more questions, then it is good enough to mail. If more do, that's great. If fewer do, go back to the drawing board.

If people think your ad is "pretty," if they think that it's "neat," or anything like that, go back to the drawing board. If they ask you questions about what you are offering, you are hitting the right things, and you are beginning to not be boring.

Strategy 33:
Get in the newspaper

Whenever you make a change in your business or do a charity function, you should try to get an article in one of the local papers about it. The purpose of this is not to create further prospects—this will not happen, believe me.

What it does is build your credibility, and this is important. When you send sales information to a prospect, you can include reprints of this article in the paper. When a prospect sees this in the paper, he automatically thinks you are for real, that your company is a good company and trustworthy.

Once a prospect thinks that you are legitimate, he will be much more likely to retain your services. Remember, people are skeptical these days. They are afraid of getting ripped off or getting poor service. Anything you do to prove to them that you are trustworthy will definitely pay off.

How do you get anything in the newspaper? Most newspaper editors call them press releases. Press releases rarely get in the newspaper. You can send them in, but the newspaper gets tons and tons of press releases. If you want to get something in the newspaper, you need to do more than send a press release. Here is how you do it.

1. Call the newspaper and find out who is in charge of press releases. Call back and ask for that person. You may have to call back several times before you get to talk to the right person.
2. Tell that person that you are sending him or her some very exciting information. Tell him or her who you are and what you do.

3. Tell him why he will benefit and/or how his readers will benefit. Here is a great way to offer your FREE tree health or hazard evaluation or FREE seven-point landscape audit.
4. Send him the information. Make sure you spell out that you talked to him on the phone and told him you were sending this. Also make it crystal clear what he gets out of this: that it is something valuable to give his readers, such as I mentioned above.
5. Follow up. Call him back and see if he received your information. Ask if he is going to put it in the paper. If he will not give you a direct answer, ask him when he will know for sure. Then call him back.
6. Be persistent.

This strategy takes effort, but it is worth it. If you really want to get in the paper, you will have to do this. Be very enthusiastic over the phone. Be friendly and cheerful. This will help you out a lot. Always expect that the newspaper will run your information. If you expect it, then generally, it will.

Strategy 34:
Write a book or report

Sound difficult? It's not. You already know the information. You just have to put it into words.

Why write a book or report? Well, if someone writes a book or report on a subject, it puts them in a different light, and that light is expertise. No longer will you just be a tree or landscape service, you'll be a tree or landscape service *expert*.

A tree or landscape rep or arborist is looked at as a salesperson. A tree or landscape expert is looked at as a person with a solution to a prospect's problems.

This makes all the difference in the world.

If you're thought of as a salesperson, prospects will back away from you. They will take what you say with a grain of salt. Even if you have the perfect solution to their needs, it'll be difficult to convince them of that. But if you're seen as an expert, you're trusted.

A prospect is coming to you with a problem, and thinks you're the person who can help him solve that problem. He'll take your advice seriously and do what you tell him to do. Do you see why this is powerful?

What to write a book or report on? That's a good question. Write on what you know. Here are some possibilities:

- How to best prune trees.
- How to avoid tree or landscape rip-offs.
- How to choose an honest tree or landscape service company.

- How to reduce the risk of poisonous pests in your home.
- The seven things to do to make your tree live and thrive twice as long.

This should be what your titles look like. The title has to create interest on the part of your prospect. A title is really a headline for the book or the report.

Of course, at the end of the book or report, you make an offer, like a free tree-care evaluation. Tell them exactly what you want them to do.

You can offer this report or book for free in all sorts of places. For example:
- In your Yellow Pages ad.
- In your ValPak or money mailer ad.
- In your newspaper column.
- Through real-estate agents.

There are many, many places to offer this information.

Become an expert. Write a book or report. We put out one called *How Not to Be Scammed by a Tree or Landscape Company*—it's very popular. And we use it in almost all of our marketing.

Strategy 35:
Write a column

You could have a newspaper or magazine column of your own.

You've seen doctors and mechanics have them—why not tree or landscape services?

In your column, you would answer questions that have been sent in. Of course, you have tons of time to write a brilliant answer.

How do you benefit from a column?

First of all, when you have your own column, you're considered an expert in the area. For years, I've seen a horticulturist with her own column. She answers tricky problems, but everyone thinks she's the brightest and best horticulturist there is. She gets tons of business from this. Whenever someone has a difficult lawn, plant, or garden problem, they immediately think of her.

Wouldn't it be nice if you were thought of when anyone in your area wanted to get service done?

Well, you bet it would, and you'd have tons of business, plus you could use this in all your marketing materials. Do you think this would help extend your credibility?

It absolutely would.

What about the people who write in for answers? Who do you think they're going to look to for tree or landscape advice and service?

Well, you, of course.

How do you get a column? It's not easy, but it's not all that hard either. First you have to really want one—that's the important part.

Don't do this if you're not completely sure.

You must get in touch with the editor of the newspaper or magazine. Call him and tell him your idea. Tell him specifically how his publication would benefit, and explain how readers would benefit from your service.

Then send a powerful sales letter, explaining all of that.

Remember to establish your credibility.

If you've done anything with charities or other organizations, include that.

Next, follow up with it.

Next, be persistent. If you're persistent and don't give up, you'll get a column, and let me know when you do, because it's very exciting when you get your first column.

Strategy 36:
Get best use from the Yellow Pages

Owners of tree and landscape companies tell me all the time that the Yellow Pages don't work, or most companies say the Yellow Pages don't work.

This is absurd—the Yellow Pages *do* work.

If they aren't working for you now, I'll teach you how to make the Yellow Pages very, very profitable.

Why do so many tree or landscape companies fail with the Yellow Pages? Take a good look at the Yellow Pages ads in your city—pull out your Yellow Pages, and look at all the tree and landscape companies' ads.

Now try to be objective.

Do you notice something? They all look pretty much alike, and say pretty much the same thing.

You could easily change the business information on all of them and they'd be the same.

None of them stand out. They all look like blown-up business cards. None of them gives any compelling reason why you should use a certain company.

Name, rank, and serial number; name, rank, and serial number; name, rank, and serial number.

BLAH, BLAH, BLAH!

Most Yellow Pages reps don't know anything about getting new clients. Stop listening to your Yellow Pages rep.

He sells everyone else their Yellow Pages and he gives your competition the same advice. That's why all the ads look the same.

After I teach you how to get a Yellow Pages ad that really works, the last thing you want to do is tell your Yellow Pages rep.

If you do, he's going to tell your competitors. Tell him that you're doing okay. Don't sound excited at all, and hopefully none of the competitors do the same thing you're doing.

And as I said, they probably won't.

Yellow Pages advertisement isn't any different than any other type of advertising. You need all the same things that we've already talked about:

1. You need attention-getting headlines.
2. You need to generate interest—say or offer something that interests the prospect.
3. Make the prospect want what you're offering.
4. Tell them the offer and exactly what to do.
5. You can even put an expiration date. Of course that can't be a specific day, for obvious reasons. Something like "expires in fifteen days" is okay, but doesn't have much effect, because people realize you have no idea when they first saw the ad.

The number-one mistake that all tree and landscape services make is using their company name as a headline.

Why would that want to make them go any further? Six out of ten people who look up a tree or landscape services in the phone book have no company in mind—that's what stats tell us—and out of the remaining four, half of them are willing to be swayed to a different company. That's eight out of ten; practically no one is looking for your name.

It's a huge waste of space to make your name the biggest thing. Instead, bring an attention-getting headline.

Anything would be better than your company name, which no one is looking for or no one will recognize. Here are other mistakes everyone makes:

1. "Certified Arborist" or "Certified Landscape Professional." Only we tree and landscape folks know what this is. If you want to use this, you must explain what kind of certification and how this benefits the client.
2. "Free estimates." Everyone does this—people expect it. It isn't anything special.
3. Fancy equipment. Only tree or landscape folks know or care the name of any fancy cherry-picker or boom truck and what this means. You must explain it—tell them why it's the best method, which should be how the client benefits from it. How does the thing that you have, equipment and such, benefit the client?

Remember, why should anyone do business with you versus any or all other of your competitors? Answer this question in your Yellow Pages ad, and you'll get tons of calls.

Why do it alone? Go to www.*treecaresuccess.com* and sign up for membership in my "Millionaire Maker" Inner Circle Program.

Strategy 37:
Use traveling billboards

Use your equipment and trucks as traveling billboards. This is absolutely free advertising.

Make the signs as large as possible.

Keep equipment sparkling clean.

Include in your message a reason to call you on all your vehicles, such as a strong guarantee. Your USP—the reason to call you instead of the competition.

Stay away from standard logo, phone number, logo, phone number, logo, phone number—it's boring and ineffective. Name, rank, and serial number. Name, rank, and serial number.

Put something on your trucks that gives potential clients a reason to call you, and you're going to be blown away at the response.

We do thousands of dollars each year just off the advertisement on our trucks.

Strategy 38:
Double your response from mailer services

Valpak or similar mailers to consumers are what most tree or landscape companies use to get new business.

Unfortunately, most use the low-price package of advertising. They advertise low, low prices.

The problem with this is that even though many consumers haven't called these ads, they believe they can get their service for a ridiculously low price.

This is a problem, but you can overcome it.

First of all, only advertise in high-end areas. Know where these ads are being delivered. Know which areas you advertise in.

Advertising price isn't enough. It may work for huge companies that everyone in America has heard of, but not for you. These companies have had more than ten years of multi-million-dollar TV campaigns behind them, so they can advertise two cheese pizzas for $9.99 and get a response. You don't have that behind you, so your ads have to be better.

The same rules apply for getting a good Valpak-type ad as for any direct-response ad: **You've got to do it differently.**

You've got to go back to our rules on emotional direct-response mailings to get response.

That is, give them a compelling reason to call you over anyone else. Yes, I keep saying that. Because it's very important when you advertise—they have to have a compelling reason to call you over any other alternative.

Strategy 39:
Send out a newsletter

A monthly or quarterly newsletter is a very easy and cheap way to keep in constant contact with your client.

Every month that you don't contact the client, he loses 10 percent of the value of your relationship. So if you don't contact your client for ten months, it's all over. That's why so many businesses lose clients.

A monthly, bimonthly, or quarterly newsletter is one of the best ways of keeping your relationship with your clients intact, and even strengthening it. I'd suggest you do one no less than six times a year.

Quarterly's a bit of a stretch. Monthly's better, but you certainly want to make sure it's at least every other month to keep in contact with these clients. You'll be rewarded greatly if you do that.

Why is a newsletter so powerful?

1. It develops a relationship between you and your clients.
2. It keeps you at the top of your client's consciousness.
3. It gives you a chance to sell something else. A newsletter is a great way to introduce new products or services.
4. It gives you a chance to continually educate your clients.
5. You can recognize clients who have referred others to you. This will increase the number of referrals you get. Once a client sees others refer you, he will usually do the same.

A newsletter, at least quarterly (and I would say at least every other month) is a must. This is an essential ingredient to keeping clients. Everything else works around this newsletter.

I highly recommend that you write your own newsletter; let your personality shine through. But if not, we can certainly do it for you. We have a service that we offer, either quarterly, every other month, or monthly, in which we send your newsletter to you, ready to go—just plug in your name, change it if anything needs to be changed, and get it out. It's that important to get these newsletters out.

Once you begin to do it, you should never stop it.

You're going to see the profit and the benefit to it.

It's also a tremendous prospecting tool that we use. If you're going in to target or farm a new area, target them with newsletters.

A major rule concerning newsletters: Don't make them too technical. Don't write like a tree or landscape professional person would write.

We did that for many years—that's ineffective.

You'll get some results that way, but you won't get nearly the results you'll get if you write it in their language, and assume they don't know what you're talking about.

We talk the language, so we put it in our newsletter and assume they're impressed with it—they're not.

They won't read it.

If you want proof on that, if you get a newsletter from your bank, or your CPA, and your financial people—do you sit and read that?

In most cases, no.

You'll flip through it and it usually goes in the trash.

Now, at least, they make contact with you, but you weren't interested in what they have to say in their newsletter because it was techno stuff.

So you want at least 60 to 70 percent of your newsletter to be things that interest the homeowner.

The clients who most tree and landscape reps are meeting with are probably 70 to 80 percent women. You need to understand that, and write things that they're interested in. It doesn't even have to be about tree or landscape. It can be a lot of different things that we throw in the newsletter of interest to them, and that way they'll look forward to it.

We put trivia in it. Every time they get it, they love to read it.

Include a brightly colored sales letter insert in most newsletters, promoting a product or service. I also use this in slow periods for any specials I might be having at a particular time.

So a newsletter is something that you certainly must have. And if you can't do it yourself, give me a call and I'll go over the pricing. It's done for you every month, or every other month, your choice.

It can be time-consuming, but it's one of the greatest things you'll ever do as far as profit and also as far as cementing a relationship with your clients.

Strategy 40: Advertise

What is the purpose of advertising?

To get new clients? No.

The purpose of advertising is to get new clients *to give you referrals*, and those referrals will give you referrals. That's where the real profits are, but to get new clients, you need to advertise.

You should advertise consistently. You want to always bring in new clients that refer others to you.

To do this successfully, you have to keep new clients coming in. In theory, you could eventually just live off referrals, but this is dreaming. No one ever gets to the point of working only from referrals, so you have to keep those new clients coming in.

If you stop or take a break, you'll get fewer new clients, you'll get fewer referrals, and pretty soon, you won't have any work.

So you have to keep advertising.

You must NOT wait until you NEED business to advertise.

Keep your funnel full of suspects and prospects!

Strategy 41:
Do you really believe folks keep your business card?
Or ... **_Do you believe they use your business card?_**

Everybody has business cards. But the question is—how do you use yours? Do you leave them in a drawer collecting dust or wrapped up with a rubber band? Or do you love giving them out? (And even get a little giddy saying, "Let me give you my card.")

As a tree or landscape business owner, your card is a vitally important business-building tool. But it's so rarely used to its full potential.

Your business card is an incredible way to earn new business, and keep clients coming back, but ... most people design it so it hardly does a thing!

More often than not, after you hand someone your card, it gets tucked in a wallet, never to see the light of day again. It's pocketed, creased, and worn. It's drowned in the laundry. It's scorched in the dryer. It's put in a desk drawer.

The list goes on.

And yet, a simple change to your card can actually keep it out of the trash *and make it very likely to generate new customers and referrals!*

What's the secret?

Your business card is NOT a contact card. It's an emotional direct-response little ad!

What's the difference? Basically, it needs to include just a headline and an offer.

Every ad you run—a sales letter, a Yellow Pages ad, a flyer, a Valpak ad—needs both.

As a business owner, your business card is no different.

You should develop an "irresistible FREE offer" which is responsible for more new business than *any* other technique out there.

Give the person who accepts your business card a **reason to WANT to keep it**. Offer them the same great deal you advertise in the Yellow Pages: the same FREE consumer report, the same "tree health care evaluation (regularly $xxx.xx)," the same FREE "tree hazard audit," or FREE "landscape consultations (reg. $xxx.xx)." You'd be amazed how much of an incentive it is to keep your card handy.

It then becomes a coupon—and people KEEP coupons!

They stick it on their fridge or tack it up in their office instead of sticking it in a drawer or throwing it in the trash.

The words, "call now for _____," or "this card is good for _____" will multiply the amount of business your business card generates. And every time you hand out the card, verbally extend the offer. Tell your prospects why they should keep that card handy.

If you're handing out cards to the right people (targeted and in the market for what you sell), you'll be amazed at how many more people actually call you back.

Next, replace any slogan with a headline, highlighting one major benefit your company offers over the competition—whether it be a guarantee, FREE sample, written industry standard specs, etc., etc., etc.

Give them one more reason they should keep that card and call *you* first.

Your name, logo, and telephone number does not make the phone ring, and that's where most business cards FAIL!

Select the benefit your clients respond to most favorably, and work that under your company name instead of that cute slogan.

Strategy 42:
Don't be an advertising victim.

An advertising victim is someone who has no plan, and makes advertising decisions based upon whether an advertising rep catches them that day.

Even if you do good direct-response ads—not those old image-building or price-driven ads, even if you do have good ads that get response, you need to have a plan (go back and reread Strategy 1).

You can't just wait for the next advertising rep to come sell you advertising. You have to plan, and you have to budget.

The other part of being an advertising victim is listening to the advertising reps about how to advertise. They'll tell you that you should do what everybody else is doing.

That stuff doesn't work.

You more than likely have learned this the hard way by doing it over and over, and it never worked for you. I've been there, and it never worked for me.

Advertising reps get really nervous if you want to use a good direct-response ad. It's different, and it makes them nervous. They will try to convince you not to do it. They'll tell you it won't work. They'll tell you it's not traditional. They'll tell you anything so you won't use it. Don't listen to them.

This stuff works. This stuff really works, but don't try to convince the advertising rep of that. Then he'll tell all of your competitors your secrets. You don't want this.

Plus, some places will even raise your advertising price if they know you're doing well. So never act like you just made $2,000 or more from the $200 ad. If he asks, tell him it did okay. If you keep running the ad because it's doing great, he still won't figure it out. He'll assume that you're crazy and wasting your money. Let him think that.

Let him think you're crazy, but don't be an advertising victim.

Strategy 43:
Master newspaper advertising

Newspaper advertising is one of the hardest media to make work. It won't make you a fortune, but it will do this: It will get you new clients.

These new clients will at least cover the cost of the ad.

But the real key is to get referrals from these new clients. Referrals are the entire reason you advertise. Referrals are much cheaper and where the real profits are.

If you don't have a system for getting referrals from clients, don't advertise. Take the time to create a referral system and then advertise. See Section 3 for strategies about referral systems.

Here are a few rules about newspaper advertising:

1. Make your ad look as close to a real article as possible. This is called an "advertorial." Editorial content is read 500 percent more than ads are. So it only makes sense that if your ad looks like a genuine article, it'll get read more.
2. Tell something newsworthy. Your content should have a very strong headline, or you won't get any response. The article should address something that people will be interested in.
3. Make a free offer. Don't try to sell anything in the newspaper. Offer a free report, recorded message, or a free tree or landscape audit or tree-care evaluation, but don't try to sell anything.

4. Bigger ads pull better than smaller ads, even if they're more expensive.

So, newspaper advertising can be a great medium for getting new clients, and basically buying clients very cheaply, but you have to use the same type of rules when it comes to writing emotional direct response when you write that ad. It's not going to look like everybody else's ad. It's going to be an editorial-type ad that gives people a very compelling reason to call you.

Customer service

Strategy 44:
Understand the lifetime value of a client

The name of this strategy gives the concept away. It is so simple that you will be dumbfounded so many people have never been this considerate.

Here is what it is all about: By definition, the LVC (or lifetime value of a client) is a total profit produced by the average client over his or her lifetime association with you.

All right, once you know your average client's lifetime value, you are then in a position to make a judgment on how much you can afford to spend to convert a prospect to a client.

For example, let's say the first time your average new client does business with you, she spends $600. She has you prune her trees every year, and is going to be a client for four years. In four years, she will have spent a minimum of $2,400 with you. Now you have to figure out how much of that profit is to you. Let's say it's 20 percent. So you theoretically will make $480 profit on your average client over the next four years.

So the question is, how much are you willing to pay to get a client? You could spend up to $480 and still break even in four years. I don't suggest that, but up to $50 certainly seems reasonable. Would you not invest $50 to get $400 back in four years?

But you don't have to wait the full four years to start getting it back. On the first sale, you make money, more than enough to cover the $50. Let's say that your average client refers at least one other client to you. Now your profit from that client is $960; $480 from the client and $480 from the referral. Referrals from your clients are much more profitable than clients who come from advertising. They are pretty much pre-sold, and so, they are very good clients.

Start calculating the lifetime value of your average client. One of your goals should be to increase this value by getting your clients to refer more often, increasing the average sale, making repeat services more often through continuity programs, and selling them more products.

Strategy 45:
They are clients, not customers

Now this is a subtle point that can make a big difference. Stop using the word "customer." Start using the word "client." Why? Because the word *customer* implies that they buy things from you, but *client* implies a close relationship in which you help the client solve problems.

As a tree or landscape service provider, you are a problem-solver. It changes the way your client sees you and also changes the way you see the client.

You are there to correct a problem or provide beauty or peace of mind on a continuous basis. They will respect you more, and vice versa, you will respect them more. After all, your clients are your most valuable asset in the business. Without them, you simply would not be in business.

Start calling them clients to your employees, so that your employees use the word *client* also. Use the word *client* in all your letters to show and establish relationships where you are there to consistently help them.

Customers are just people who buy from you, and who may or may not ever buy from you again.

I have noticed that people tend to think of customers as nuisances. They are people who come in and violate your time.

Clients are important, and they are treated as such. Start using the term *client* and you will see that your clients will take to this also.

Strategy 46:
Remember that you are not the client

This is a mistake that many, many business owners make. Especially tree and landscape companies.

What this means is that you do not know what your clients will want or how they're going to react.

Lots of tree and landscape companies will say, "Well, my clients won't like this or respond to that." This is a huge mistake. Remember, you are not the client. You don't know what your client will or won't do until you try it. Don't try to spend their money.

Please don't ever say, "This will never work with my clients." First of all, that's very foolish. You don't know what will or what won't work with your clients. Second of all, these marketing strategies have been tested all over the country. They work—period. This will be like questioning the law of aerodynamics every time a plane crashes. No one does that. They ask what was wrong with the plane or what mistake the pilot made.

If you can't get something to work, give me a call. I'll help you to get it to work. If you have problems, don't say, "I tried this and it doesn't work." What you should say is, "I tried this, and I couldn't get it to work," or even better yet, "I tried this, and I couldn't get it to work. Do you know how I can get it to work?" Then I can explain what you're doing wrong, so you can correct it.

Do not end up losing thousands and thousands of dollars because you are so sure this didn't work—start small, work your way up, and always remember that you aren't your own client. Let the client make up his own mind.

Strategy 47:
Wow your clients

You want your client to be *in awe* after doing business with you. Does it sound hard? It may, be but it is really easy.

It is easy because most businesses do a lousy job. They do not even do what they are supposed to do.

Of course, most don't do anything extra, so it is easy for you to stand out.

What do you do to "WOW" your client? Let's go over a few things—a free coffee mug, 99 cents is all they cost; free refrigeration calendar—50 cents. Ball caps—$2 to $4.

As you can see, it is very cheap to "WOW" a client this way. Our best, most effective way we "WOW" our clients is with a freebie. I teach my people to add free items to the client's job ticket. Small things that do not cost anything, or they cost very little, but have high perceived value to the client.

Let me give you a few ways we do it with small things that do not cost anything or very little, but have high perceived value to the client. Here are some examples:

- Clean out the extra flower bed area (that you have to clean out anyway).
- Pick up the raking from their weekend yard job.
- Prune an extra small tree.
- Clean out their gutters while you are already on the roof.

The list can go on and on and on. Make sure your clients are very aware of the free service you gave them.

Put it on your work order, or invoice it at no charge or free. Just write it on there: free, we did this for you.

Our clients love this. We get rave comments from our clients about this. Your clients will feel very special.

Do you think your clients will ever go anywhere else to get their trees trimmed? Not on your life. They will be loyal as they can be.

Why don't more companies do this? Most companies look at this as expense.

Now this is stupid!

It is the cheapest and easiest way to get repeat business and a lot of referrals, but most do not look at the whole picture, they just look at the cost. This is ridiculous, but you and I can really benefit from their shortsightedness.

"In a blind man's world, the one-eyed man is king."

You don't have to be super great. You only have to be *better* than the competition, which is not that tough to do these days.

But if it is a cost problem with you, then what you want to do when you set up your budget is to budget this in. It is simply a cost of doing business; no different than any other marketing or advertising cost.

Make it your mindset.

So you have to remember **"If you want to get what you want, you have to see to it that other people get what they want."**

That's an old marketing cliché, but it is certainly true.

Again, if you help someone else get what they want, they will see to it you get what you want.

It really works.

Strategy 48:
Cater to your dream clients

You have what you call your top clients, right? They're giving you a ton of business. These dream clients are giving you the most business. They can be a homeowner, a golf course, or a firm. They can be a group of residential customers.

Pick the ones out of your database (you do have one, don't you?) who are giving you all this business.

At least once a month or so, gift them, send them a report, or make some sort of contact. It may just be a phone call. They will increase the amount of times they use your service or refer you if you do this. It's very important.

You treat these people differently because they are the ones who are giving you a tremendous amount of your sales and profits.

So keep on top of them.

You want to make sure the arborist or yourself (if you are the one who's doing the selling and working with these clients) get by their homes periodically.

You leave a card and let them know you were there.

Keep these people on the top of your mind.

Make sure your receptionist and the people who work in your office know who these clients are. When they call in, they're not put on hold. When they call in, they get top-notch service.

You should run over yourself for these people because these people, who are generally the top 20 percent of your client database, are the ones giving you the most revenue and **profits!**

Strategy 49:
Cater to your dream referral clients

This could be some folks that you've never worked for, but they are sending a lot of referrals to you.

You want to do the same strategy for them as you do your dream clients. It keeps them referring. So keep gifting them.

Basically, they are unpaid salespeople in the marketplace working for you, so it only makes sense that you reward them. It does not have to be very expensive stuff. They just want to be acknowledged.

For most people, it doesn't matter the monetary value. What matters is being recognized.

When you call them or you go by their home (and they know you've been there), and you leave a card with a note thanking them for thinking of your company, it means a lot to them. Gifts that you send them work the same way. They have high perceived value.

You may not pay much for them, but their perceived value to that client is high.

It makes a tremendous difference.

Set up a system so you don't forget to do this.

They will refer you and be "clients for life." It's all in the relationship!

Strategy 50:
Constantly educate your clients

Never assume that your clients will remember. You need to constantly educate them about your company, product information, material information, maintenance, etc.

After the first time a tree or landscape company services a client's home, he usually never educates the clients any more after that, if he did it at all. A tree or landscape owner or arborist assumes the client knows it. This is a gigantic mistake.

It takes time to learn. If you saw a client every twelve months, and even if you did a great job in educating them (which is doubtful), they still wouldn't remember much. Remember, just because trees and landscapes are your life doesn't mean it's everyone else's. It's certainly not your clients'. People forget—it's natural.

You must constantly educate your clients over and over.

And if by chance one of them says, "Yeah, I know that" and goes on to explain it, you say, "Oh, I'm sorry—most of our clients don't have a great memory about trees and landscapes like you do."

This rarely happens, but even if it does, people smile. They feel special and bright, and that's great. Your goal should be to get all of your clients to say that—then you'll be doing a good job. Better yet, your bank account will be overflowing.

You should have information packets explaining all aspects of tree care and other services you offer. You don't need to bombard your clients with everything at once. A constant flow of information to them from you is best.

How do you accomplish this?

Well, you can do it several ways, but one is through your monthly newsletter or quarterly newsletter. ISA or NAA educational material. Sales letters. When you're actually at their home, talk to them about it.

Every one of your clients should have a general knowledge of all the services you offer.

It's silly to have most of your clients using only one or two of your services. It's much cheaper and more profitable to get most of your clients to use most of your services.

This only happens through constant education.

Strategy 51:
Set up a lending library

A lending library is another thing you can give to your clients. It's another way to "WOW" them.

It is a list of books that you have that you are willing to lend to your clients.

Now, these books should relate to home improvement and your tree or landscape services:

Books that will help them fix up the home, save money, make life easier.

Books about lawn maintenance and tree care.

Books about other services.

Any information that could be helpful to them.

In other words, not your tree or landscape business manuals, which have no value to your clients. But things they would appreciate.

You can also stress that you're really into consumer education, and offer all sorts of books about:

- How to save money on taxes, or any tax information.
- How to buy your dream house.
- Anything that is designed to educate the consumer.

Stick to things that most of your clients have or do.

For example, they all have to do taxes. Then inform your clients that you have a lending library in your new client kit, which of course is presented at your initial meeting.

Of course, you will have to choose your own books, reports, tapes, whatever you want to offer, for your lending library.

Make sure all your books in the lending library agree with the way that you do things; for example, if you use odorless, environmentally friendly materials, you want to make sure that the books and stuff you give out goes along with that type of material.

So, the way the lending library works is this:

You can borrow any of the items for one month, free of charge. You can drop off the request or mail it.

And when finished, your customer has to simply drop the item back off at your office or pay for the postage to send it back.

Remember, the items in your lending library are mainly designed to help educate the consumer in awareness of tree care, pest control, landscape services. And then, of course you can expand your lending library to include other consumer information on taxes, buying a home, etc.

And don't forget to stress that only *your clients* have the privilege of the lending library.

And, again—be sure and put your contact information on all the books you lend. If they pass them around or copy them, you want them to keep "selling" for you.

Strategy 52:
Send thank-you letters

Thank-you letters bring in a positive feeling about your company. When was the last time you received a thank-you from someone you did business with? Most businesses just don't bother with it.

Thank-you letters are very important and are often overlooked by tree or landscape companies. For less than fifty cents a letter, you create a good feeling for your company. This is one of the cheapest ways that you can build trust and a chance to get more referrals. You should use a form or thank-you card. You should send it out the day after the job. This is very easy. You just add the person's name, sign, and mail.

Simple, cheap, easy—and very effective.

A thank-you card left at the home when you finish the job just doesn't cut it. It doesn't look or feel personal. In my view, to have any impact, the client must feel special. Your "thank-you" reinforces that you are a wonderful company and that your clients need to get their trees cared for regularly. Get it. Use it. Systematize it and use it consistently.

Here is another: Send a "thank-you," even if you did not sell the client. It is a little different than most do. Always send a thank-you card immediately, within twenty-four hours, after you present a proposal and you didn't sell it. You will be amazed at the ones you will sell just by this courteous gesture.

Even if you do not sell it, you have built tremendous good will with this prospect for the future. If the tree company that gets the job messes up, who do you think will get the job next time? You, of course. You always want to come in as number two if you can't get the job.

We all know that a lot of tree-care companies and landscape companies and lawn services do not do good work. So you are positioned as number two for them to fall back on once they are not happy with the other service.

And, as you know, that happens quite a bit in our business.

Strategy 53:
Give workshops

Workshops are designed to create an interest in your service. It's a good strategy to use if you open up in a new area, or you want to build up an area. It's a very good strategy to do, and not enough people do it.

A workshop is designed to create interest in your services. You want to have prospects attend, but that can be a problem in itself. You cannot advertise in the newspaper for a free workshop. This doesn't work. It's too expensive, and barely anyone will show up.

So how do you get prospects to attend?

You go through organizations, clubs, and associations. You give a workshop specially designed for them. This gets their members interested in your services, and many attendees will become clients. This won't cost you much. The organization will supply the meeting room. They should tell all their members through meetings and newsletters. So since this doesn't cost them anything, they don't mind doing this. I can tell you by experience, they don't. But you should supply them with the material you will be using and passing out.

For example, if you're going to put an article in their monthly newsletter, you should write it and give it to them. If they're going to announce it at a meeting, you should write the announcement. Don't ask them to do it. If you let them do it, you'll get little response. The people won't show up. You have to present the announcement in an interesting way so the members are interested. You can either have the organization take reservations, or you can.

Usually, the organization is willing to do this, but not always. Just ask them. Make sure you have a deadline of at least one week in advance for them to sign up. This way you'll be able to prepare the amount of handouts and different things that you're going to give out for free.

Okay, how to get into the organization?

Call the organization and ask for the person in charge of educational programs.

You must tell them how the organization will benefit, or else they won't be interested at all.

The best way is to donate to the organization a certain percentage of all the work you get because of the workshop, let's say 5 percent. And also offer a discount to all their members of $25 off or 10 percent, something like that—a set amount of dollars always works better. This way, the organization can see if they will be making money and be offering something valuable to their members.

Ask the person if you can come over to discuss a workshop with them. On the phone, just tell them that you have a way to help them make money for their organization. Most people in these types of organizations would be more than happy to give you a few minutes of their time. Explain the whole thing to them, and tell them what exactly their members will learn, even if they don't use any of your services.

Some of the best organizations to go to are churches and synagogues. Other ones that have a high senior citizen membership are good too.

Senior citizens usually have to hire someone to trim their trees, and they're more worried about thoroughness. They usually can afford your services also.

Garden clubs are very good prospects.

At the actual workshop, you can focus on different things for different organizations, whatever they're most interested in.

A few examples are specific pest problems, how infestation takes place, how to plant and care for your trees, or how to prune your small trees.

Obviously, your presentation should really emphasize getting their trees cared for on a regular basis. If you give them the information, they're going to use your services, not someone else's.

Then, offer all the attendees a free tree-care evaluation if they sign up that day. Plus, if they do use any services, they'll get a discount for being a member of the organization.

It's important that you get everyone to fill out an evaluation form, or make sure you get everyone's name and address.

For just an hour of your time, think how much business you'll generate. You should get at least—this is bare minimum, four new clients, with an average job of $400 to $600—at our office here, our average job price is right at $900. But if it's just $400 to $600, that's $1,600 to $2,400 for an hour's worth of work, and let me tell you, that's not bad.

Plus, everyone who doesn't sign up immediately for the free evaluation receives a sales letter. And you should average at least three referrals per client. That's twelve referrals. You see why this is so profitable. Your out-of-pocket cost is virtually zero.

You can also do workshops for real-estate agents. They have many clients who purchase homes, but don't have a tree or landscape expert to take care of them. You offer to give the real-estate agent a percentage of the sales from the workshop, and offer his or her clients a discount. Because this is a valuable thing they're giving their clients, they should be willing to tell them for free.

You must convince the real-estate agents that their clients will love them for giving a valuable workshop, and they'll refer lots of new clients to them. Plus, they'll choose the agents again if they ever choose to move to a new home. Otherwise, you can split the cost of mailing with them. You'll still make lots of money from this workshop, so you can afford it.

Make sure you write all the information, just like any other sales letter. Don't let the real-estate agent to it.

Now, as an aside, here's what I do. We get a lot of speaking engagements. I take different organizations and begin to mail them our newsletter. We put them on our newsletter lists, and on our prospect lists. We mail to organizations such as garden clubs, any type of green industry organizations, tree organizations, plant organizations, and horticultural societies. These sorts of organizations are always looking for experts to speak at their meetings.

I said you can expect four clients, but don't be surprised when you've got a meeting of thirty or forty people, and you get ten or fifteen clients. These tend to be bonded groups, so when someone goes for you, the other ones do, too. Once you do a good job for one, it spreads like wildfire through their organization, and you get a lot of clients. We have been very successful at getting clients this way.

I can't emphasize enough how you need to get this strategy going. If nothing else, get your newsletter going, and start mailing it to the horticultural societies, the garden clubs, the churches, and all these organizations.

Get a list of them.

Mail these people.

Mail every two or three months, the more often the better, and you're going to be blown away by them calling you and wanting to know if you can speak at their meeting coming up.

Strategy 54:
Give a big, bold, solid guarantee

You should guarantee every job you do.

Your first reaction might be, "I can't afford to do that. I'll get people calling me all the time to trim their trees again, or they will want their money back and rip me off."

This is a natural reaction, but completely untrue. This is our guarantee. In bold headlines, it says **"100 percent 'No Risk' guarantee."** Here is how it reads:

> As the owner, I want you to be super pleased, and in fact, absolutely delighted with every tree or landscape job I do. So every job comes with an iron-clad, "risk-free" guarantee. What does that mean? Simply this: If you are unhappy with the work, I will redo the items in question. If you are still unhappy, you do not owe me a dime for that item, not one red cent, no hard feelings. It is your choice. Many companies do not guarantee their work, but I do. Nothing is more important than your complete and total satisfaction. I stand behind every job 100 percent. If you ever have any questions or concerns about the work, please call me right away.

This comes with my picture on it and also me signing it, so I mean it. Is it bold? Yes. Is this strong? Yes. Is this risky?

Not at all.

Think about it this way:

My tree-care firm only gave money back approximately four times in the last five years—and that was because I decided to and not because the client asked for it. I felt I could not live up to their expectations, so I basically fired them. That is not very many. I would have done this without a written guarantee.

But do you know how many people who are hesitant and went with us because of that guarantee? Tons of them. Because I have such a strong guarantee, people think I am completely competent in my work, which I am, and they develop trust.

I do not think anyone should be in business if they do not guarantee their work. If you are not competent in what you do, do something in which you are competent. The numbers work in your favor to offer a strong, strong guarantee. It is very rare that anyone will take you up on it, but lots of people will be convinced to use you if you have one.

Once you develop a guarantee, use it. Use it in all your marketing advertising. Tell all your clients. If you've got it, flaunt it.

If you look at our trucks, you will find our USP which says, "The Most Thorough Tree Care *Ever* ... or it's FREE!" It is on our bid sheets. It is on all of our marketing stuff, because it is a tremendous marketing tool when it comes to selling jobs.

Some of the greatest reasons that people do not hire tree or landscape firms (this is from a survey that was put out by the NAA many years ago) are:

- They are not comfortable with us.
- They do not know what they are going to get.
- They do not know how the trees are going to look.

There are a lot of unknowns. This guarantee puts them in their comfort zone. It simply allows them to hire us, knowing that if anything is not what it should be, then they simply do not have to pay us.

Let me ask you a question: If someone you work for is not happy with your work, will you go back and redo it for them? Well, the answer is probably yes. If they are still very unhappy, are you still going to charge them? The answer is probably no.

The worst thing you want is a client in a neighborhood where you do work badmouthing you because of something they did not like, even if it was your fault. You want to take that bad taste out of their mouth because it is awfully difficult for someone to tell their neighbors a bad thing about you if they have never paid you a dime; in fact, you worked for them FREE!

This is one of my preemptive strategies in selling.

Here is what I mean by that.

You have bid a job and didn't sell it. You call the client back later that evening or the next day (which you had better be doing), or they call you back.

They decided to go with Suzie Jones Tree and Landscape Company. Here's the "take-away" strategy, a very strong strategy. What I call my pre-emptive strategy.

Ask them, "May I ask you about their guarantee? Do they have one?"

The prospect says, "Well, sure they have one."

"How was it written? What does it say?" As you know and I know, very few have written guarantees. What the other company is going to tell you is, "Well, it is not in writing."

And, of course, your comment is something like, "It's not in writing? You mean they are going to give you a guarantee but it is not in writing. Ours is in writing."

What that causes them to do is go back to the competition, ask them for a guarantee in writing, which in most cases, they are not going to get.

But normally, you are going to use this before it ever gets to that. But that is just one way that you use this strong guarantee out in the marketplace.

A large local newspaper in our area found out about our strong guarantee, and wrote a lengthy article about us and our guarantee.

Lots of work from that one!

Strategy 55:
Respond to complaints fast

The key to keeping and even enhancing client relations is to respond to complaints quickly and efficiently.

Never leave a client unhappy. If they are a bad apple and you want to get rid of them, give them their money back. If you give them their money back, then they can't say bad things about you. If you don't, they will go to all ends to tell everyone they know what a terrible company you are. Think of it as money well spent to save you from bad publicity.

For clients who are good clients and something just went wrong, correct it in a hurry. When you get a complaint, get to it within twenty-four hours—even sooner, if possible.

Here is what should happen to a client who complains: You respond to them and take care of them in a very timely manner. Send them a gift. Send them a second gift. Overwhelm them, no matter how small the problem is.

What you have just done is created a client for life. You've got yourself a referral machine!

Here is why:
- Now you are in their comfort zone.
- Now your guarantee is not just words.
- Now what you say is not idle tales.
- Now they know you are good.
- They know you back up what you say.
- They don't have to worry anymore.
- Now you have a good client in them from now on.

So use complaints as marketing. Use them as a marketing tool to get clients and their friends, because now they know you will take care of them.

Let's talk about frontline exposure. No matter how powerful the company's management or client satisfaction, the company profits are contingent on the actions of the company's frontline, client-exposed employees. Your frontline staff must be trained in the importance of not only satisfying the client, but WOWING them as well.

Frontline employees must be alert, creative, and empowered to break the rules if necessary to deliver high-end "WOW" service. Allow your frontline people to have the latitude to not only rectify the problems, but go overboard to satisfy the client, to bring them back for future business. A short-term loss will quickly become long-term profits.

All right. Now, let's talk about commitment to service. When a mistake is made, the staff must not only know the six-step process for saving the customer, but also fervently demonstrate the company's commitment to excellence and customer service. The six-step process for saving a dissatisfied client is this:

1. Listen.
2. Apologize.
3. Promise rectification.
4. Allow customer to assist in the fixing of the problem.
5. Fix the problem.
6. Add a free bonus element to the solution.

Listening to the customer's concerns and complaints is of paramount importance. Be polite and courteous.

Extreme courtesy usually has a soothing effect on even the gruffest customer.

Apologize for the unfortunate circumstances that have taken place. Assume all responsibility, whether your company or staff is responsible or not. Admit the mistakes or errors, and here is a big one: do not argue.

Promise rectification of the situation.

Allow the customer to tell you what they want to satisfy them in the unfortunate situation.

They often ask little to rectify the situation.

Fix the problem. Don't wait. Fix it now.

All right. Now, add a free element to the mix, a free service or product, a discount, a premium, a coupon, whatever it takes to show your sincerity and goodwill. WOW them into returning to your business.

Next, when we get things fixed (and usually not before), we send them anywhere from a $15 to $40 "we goofed" package, depending on the type of client and the amount of the ticket.

Usually it is some flowers, candies, cheeses, or whatever. We kind of mix it up.

We send it to them with a note stating to them "We goofed" but we want to keep them as a client.

Sometimes we include a little gift that includes our info on it.

We try to overwhelm them with freebies to show them that we didn't mean to mess up. We're sorry we messed up.

Like we said about complaints before, this is a great way to keep clients and cement them for life.

Now they know that you will take care of them.

Strategy 56:
Better your competition

The vast majority of consumers have grown to expect substandard or average service from tree and landscape companies.

It's a sad fact.

Today's consumers, although much more street smart, have grown to accept standard service as good.

Furthermore, they often expect substandard service. Smart marketers have taken this consumer expectation and blasted it into a marketing weapon.

I noted that in a blind man's world, the one-eyed man is king, meaning that you don't have to be great—you just have to be *better than the rest of them*, which is easy to do.

Now, the ultra-successful companies impress and capitalize by delivering knockout/wow service. They go beyond the norm, offering a high-end service coupled with unexpected perks. They practice under-promising and over-delivering.

I'll give you an example of this: You take your car in for some major service work. You're told it will cost around $400 and will be ready in about two days. What was your true gut instinct expectations? Let me guess.

1. It will likely end up costing more than $400
2. It will likely take more than two days.

You may not dwell on them, but they will exist in your mind as expectations. Most often, your initial gut expectations are found to be correct. The same thing could occur with virtually any service business.

The fact is simply this: The consumer has been let down by average service companies. Their services have been less than promised or expected.

Back to the auto repair example. Imagine receiving a call at the end of the second day. They indicate that your car was finished ahead of schedule. That would be a nice feeling, wouldn't it? Perhaps not enough to tell your friends about, but good news nevertheless.

All right. You arrive to pick up your car to find it has been washed and vacuumed. A good feeling of confidence suddenly comes over you. You then walk in the lobby and the manager hands you the service invoice telling you the final repair came in at $75 less than expected. "Wow, this place is great," you say to yourself. You leave totally impressed.

The fact that the repair was done correctly only adds to the "WOW" service. In the next day's mail, you receive a note hand-signed by the owner thanking you for trusting your auto-repair needs to their service center. Included with this letter is a courtesy coupon for 10 percent off any future service.

Double wow.

This place wins.

Not only will you never go anywhere else, but you would most likely tell many others about your unusual experience with this place. The repair shop enjoys additional business without any additional advertising expenditures.

How much did all these perks cost the company?

Practically nothing.

Just a different outlook on marketing affected their business from the customer's point of view.

It takes five times as much money in marketing to recruit a new customer as it does to keep an existing one. Treat existing customers with kindness and understanding.

What little is expended to keep them satisfied is considerably more economical than replacing them.

Most business entrepreneurs seek to capture the new customer without harnessing the marketing power of those they already have.

Remember, an important part is giving them more than they expected.

All right, now let's go back to good versus great service, and bettering your competition.

Existing clients will return if the service is good, but they will tell many others if the service is great. The flipside of this fact follows next. It's called the domino effect.

Dissatisfied clients will voice their bad experience to a dozen others. Usually that's a minimum.

Think about it.

When you were dissatisfied with a company's product or service, how many people did you tell about your experience? Studies have shown the average is between eight and sixteen. The frightening part of this statistic is that it doesn't take into consideration the domino effect, the number of others told through the grapevine.

So now let's talk about the silent boycotting.

Some 91 percent of dissatisfied customers will not communicate their negative experience to your company, but will instead simply choose not to return. For every dissatisfied customer who complains, there are nine others who will not. They will instead simply take their business elsewhere.

Develop frontline staff members. Your business can offer the very best service in the marketplace, but if your staff doesn't carry out the company's policies and customer-centered identity in every contact with a client, the business is weakened. The goal then is to empower the staff to understand the importance of their role in the company's position on "WOW" customer relations.

Advise your staff of your company's client-centered position statement. No employee wants to work in a losing or a second-rate company.

Survey your clients. Survey every client after you work for them. You'll get a wealth of information just by asking clients to let you know.

Keep those clients coming back.

Harvest any complaint or ill feeling that might happen. If not, you might never know about it.

Strategy 57:
Understand your clients' mindset

The service you offer is, in many cases, a new experience for your client. Furthermore, this experience is emotional.

Most frontline employees fail to understand this emotional mindset when in contact with a prospect or client both by phone and in person. A dentist may think of removal of your aching tooth as just another extraction, but we may think of it as a painful experience. A ski instructor thinks skiing is a fun and easy sport, but we may view it as an opportunity to break our legs. The auto body repair shop treats our wrecked car as just another repair job, but we see it as lost transportation. So you've got to see it the client's way.

Although all are professionals in their respective fields, those who can empathize with their client's mindset will stand out above most in the marketplace.

When you provide your services, understand your client's emotional state of mind. Develop understanding. You must understand the mindset of the prospect or client when they have a reason to approach your business.

Remember, a client or a prospect's confidence in your business is magnified a thousand fold when you see it as they do and demonstrate a true interest in satisfying their concerns, thereby eliminating their fears and doubts.

Understanding their mindset as well as gaining their confidence and trust is paramount to kicking off a successful business relationship. We must understand their underlying reasoning processes. We must regard our service as a benefit of our clients, not just our bank accounts. Once we understand this mindset, we can begin to better service our client and most importantly, they will recognize it.

It's like the local restaurant that may not have the finest food, but the host knows your name, seats you without reservations, and offers that little extra when it comes to service.

Again, it's your understanding of their thought process and their mindset.

Once you get in their head, then you know exactly how to make the client happy.

You get them in their comfort zone.

That's exactly where you need them. It will ensure that you keep them as clients.

And, of course, the jobs keep rolling in, and you have to keep going to the bank to deposit money!

So keep doing it.

Making new sales

Strategy 58:
Get a competitive edge by selling with pruning standards

On pruning proposals, always go by and go over the A-300 pruning standards with your prospect. These are standards, as you well know, that are in our industry.

Make for certain they get a copy.

Now, you know that most tree or landscapes know very little about these standards—and the ones who do don't use them or understand them. That gives you a giant leg up in selling.

For instance, Ms. Jones said XYZ Tree or Landscape gave a much cheaper price. I simply ask this, "May I ask what pruning standards they are using to offer such a lower price?"

Without slamming your competition, you will be requiring Ms. Jones to ask your competition the same question. It works very well closing sales.

Strategy 59:
Pay attention to the front end

The front end is what most of us think about. It is making the first sale with the prospect.

That is it—the first sale.

The subsequent sales are the back end. Why are we so engrossed in the front end? I have a tendency to believe I need more clients, and that is what I concentrate on. Obviously, getting new clients is very important, but there is another very important profit center that is called the back end.

The front end has to carry all of our advertising costs.

For example, if you run a Valpak ad and it costs $300 and you get three new clients from it, it costs you $100 to get each of those clients. If your average for those three clients was $600, then you probably made out okay, but if your average job was $50, then you lost money.

Some companies intentionally lose money on the first sale. This may sound ridiculous, but it's not.

They know the lifetime value of their clients. Therefore they know how much they can spend on a new client. They are willing to lose money on the first sale just to get that person as a client. They know that most of their new clients go on to buy more products or services from them. It is not until the second or third sale that a client is profitable. They know this and market this way. That is fine and it works.

You don't have to go that far. You can make money on the front end and make even more money on the back end. The whole point of spending advertising dollars is to obtain a new client, not a one-time-only customer, but a client who is going to use your services over and over again; that is the purpose of the front end.

For instance, let's say you want to get into a certain upscale neighborhood. You could possibly bring your price down, giving them a special price on the first-time sale. Make sure the client knows why you are doing it.

Let's say your prospect has a lot of trees. They have them pruned periodically by another firm. They buy fertilization services and all the other services that the other firm offers.

You analyze this.

You can see how over the years you could have a profitable relationship with these people.

So, let's say it's a $3,000 job.

You are going to make $600 profit off of it.

Cut your profit out of it the first time, and charge $2,400.

Take a little hit on it. Get that client to use you for all their services.

Congratulations!

You have just purchased a client for break-even.

You have added a client to your database that is going to give you a whole lot of profit down the road.

We do that to get the type of client that we want.

It is a very effective strategy to build your future profits by leaps and bounds!

Get them in your system and start making a profit from them today!

Strategy 60:
Never leave them empty-handed

You should never leave a client empty-handed. Your sales rep or arborist should never leave a client empty-handed either. If you do, you're wasting an opportunity to make more money. You can easily give them information on your other services that they aren't using.

Here's a partial list of things you can leave with your client:

1. Your referral program information.
2. Why she should get her trees pruned more often.
3. Your yearly maintenance continuity program.
4. Your tree and shrub fertilization service, if they are not using them.

Your other services may include, but are not limited to, disease and insect services, soil aeration, cabling, landscape pest control, and—this is a great add-on that we've got—gutter cleaning (you're on the roof anyway).

No matter what else you give your client, you should always give them your referral program information. You always want your client to refer. So you should encourage them to do so. If you do this, I guarantee you you're going to get more referrals.

Have you ever heard of the saying, "The squeaky wheel gets the grease?" Well, it's true. "Ask and you shall receive." Have you ever heard that? Nothing just happens—you have to make it happen. Since you don't get to see your clients very often, don't waste an opportunity to educate and sell them.

Leave them with plenty of goodies to read, listen to, or watch. This is a golden opportunity that 99 percent of tree or landscape companies miss. Join us in that 1 percent, because I guarantee you, it certainly works.

Let me help you with this.

Go to www.treecaresuccess.com and sign up for membership in my "Millionaire Maker" Inner Circle Program.

Strategy 61:
Require new prospects to meet with you when delivering a proposal

This strategy alone will drastically increase your selling percentage.

I know. They say they don't have time. It conflicts with their schedule. They say "just leave it on the door."

You're asking for trouble. If you do that, you are just another piece of paper, and you had better be the cheapest or you will never sell it.

Don't worry; once you explain why you need them there, it is easy.

Let me give you a quick example. You go to the prospect's home. You've got a nice truck or vehicle. You're dressed very well. You are very professional. You spend thirty or forty minutes on the property writing up the proposal, making sure that you are able to totally thrill the prospect. Make certain it is priced correctly.

They get exactly what they want.

You are very professional, and you leave your proposal. The next gentleman or lady arrives. They drive up with a truck that is rattling, and the fenders are about to fall off. They fall out the wrong side of the door, cigarette in their mouth, ashes falling off, beer on their breath, and shirt undone.

They look terrible.

But you know what? They write up a proposal, they leave it just like you left it.

The client or prospect gets home that evening and what do they see? Two pieces of paper. They don't see how good you were or how bad they were; they see two pieces of paper. What are they going to go by? They are simply going to go by price.

You spent a lot of money on marketing. So require that they be there with you, so you can really show them how your company shines. You will up your closing percentages 10, 20, or 30 percent and better—just by using this one strategy.

Strategy 62:
Let them choose between you, you, and you

Let's talk about that.

When you are selling, it is a big mistake to only have one offer. When you have one offer, the only choice is between you and your competition. You don't want this.

How do you get them to choose between you, you, and you, not between you and your competition?

It's simple. Multiple packages.

The only question is which option. I suggest having three options. You have to have at least two. What are the options?

1. Safety pruning only. That is least expensive usually.
2. Prune for cosmetic purposes only with safety (medium priced).
3. Maintenance prune, with safety prune, with deep root fertilization (a higher price).

You get the picture. You should be able to come up with your own. Once the prospect sees all three options, everyone, most likely, will choose one of them. Make sure you mention that number three is your most popular one, which in most cases it is. Make sure it is; don't tell them a misstatement, but generally, it is—if you check your records.

In fertilization, you also can offer them different programs. A one-time, twice a year, three times a year, depending on the area of the country where you operate.

In fertilization and in pruning, you always want to give them a choice. You want to give them more than one choice so they are making a choice of you, you, and you. It is a very, very effective strategy.

Strategy 63:
Be a sales superstar, and love it!

Don't hate selling. We sell every day of our lives, not just at work, but at home. You sell your spouse on all sorts of things—going out to dinner, where you want to go, rubbing your back. Your own children sell you on the idea of an ice-cream cone or an extra piece of candy.

Everyone sells every day of his life—it's a natural part of life. Maybe you never thought of it that way, but it's true. Your spouse may be harder to sell than any of your clients, but you aren't afraid of doing it. You aren't shy—so why should you be with your clients? You do it with your spouse, children, friends, and employees because you want it your way. It's the same thing with clients.

Of course, you can't insist with them. Don't confuse selling with pressuring. No one wants to be pressured. They hate it. Never pressure your clients—that's a good way to lose them. You sell by educating.

Name your service. Call it a "Tree Health Care Evaluation" or "Tree-Hazard Evaluation." Explain exactly what it does, and why it's important.

My favorite is a "Tree Care Evaluation." This covers all the situations.

Then you're ready to close the sale, explain the different options. There's a huge difference here.

The prospect feels like he's being offered something very important. The prospect will then understand what tree inspections are and why he needs them. Then ask which option he wants to go with.

Do you see the difference? I hope so, because it means doubling your average job, and therefore doubling your profit.

Handle possible objections before they come up. That way, you cover all your bases by educating and not by pressuring.

You must really understand this process.

Strategy 64:
Give evaluations, not estimates

When someone calls and asks for an estimate, say "I am sorry, we don't give estimates, but I will be thrilled to give you a Tree-Care Evaluation." Then explain exactly what a "Tree-Care Evaluation" entails.

This works beautifully. Prospects become much more interested and they place much more value on this than they do on an estimate. Everybody gives a "free estimate." I personally don't like the word "estimate." Estimate implies that you aren't exactly sure how much it is going to be. It may be higher. It may be lower.

A quote, however, is precise. This is exactly how much it will be for those services. Of course, a quote for tree service comes with our "Tree-Care Evaluation," but the prospect gets a lot more. Prospects to whom you give a "Tree-Care Evaluation" are much more likely to become clients, and then they are much more likely to become repeat clients.

After the evaluation, they understand the importance of pruning or fertilizing their trees or doing their landscape on a regular basis. If the proposal involves tree removals, offer to write and give pricing on tree-removal specifications and processes. Then give them planting ideas and specifications.

If it's pruning, write or give them pruning standards (A300).

You will be much more successful in getting the price that you require for the work that you do.

Strategy 65:
Give FREE "Tree-Hazard Evaluations"

This is a tremendous way to get a flood of new clients. Before the spring or winter storms arrive, send a letter to upscale neighborhoods. Offer to provide a free "Tree-Hazard Evaluation" on all their shade trees. At our company, this is a $135 value. This secret will get you a bunch of work and new clients.

I tested putting a price on it, instead of offering it for free. I priced it at $19.95, and explained that it was regularly a $135 value. We got more response (approximately double) by adding a price to it than we did when we offered it free.

When you are marketing for *new* prospects, it is better to give a free Tree-Hazard Evaluation or a free Tree-Health Evaluation than charge for it.

If you are marketing to your active clients, it is much better and much more effective to put a price on it. You do not want to give it away for free and make them think from now on it is a free service.

In your business, it should be a paid service that you offer.

So with your clients, you want to always put a price on it, show the savings they are getting, and you will get a tremendous result doing it that way.

Making more sales

Strategy 66:
Pay attention to the back end

This is where the real profits are. The back end is any sale after the first sale. It is the repeat sale. So, in other words, there aren't any advertising dollars spent in getting the repeat sales. That means that all the profit is truly profit.

It is much, much easier to get a client to buy a second time than it is to get a non-client to buy the first time. People are skeptical. They are afraid you are going to rip them off or do a poor job. Once they have used your services, that fear is gone. They know of you and trust you, hopefully.

Who wants a client who only gets their trees trimmed or fertilized once? You should always seek those clients who have their trees trimmed and the landscape service done on a regular and a consistent basis. Aim your marketing toward getting more of them.

The more the client buys from you, the more likely he or she will buy from you in the future. That means that a client who gets his trees trimmed every six months will be much more likely to buy fertilization or soil therapy from you than one who only gets his trees trimmed every three years.

Never underestimate the back end. It is a real profit center. Always create more things to sell to your client. Always keep an eye out for things in your client's landscape that you could add to your services, because it is very important. You are already there. The big expense is taken care of and that extra step just throws it to the bottom line.

Strategy 67:
Create a cash-flow surge

Have letters ready to go to be used for an immediate cash-flow surge when business drops drastically, such as our Texas drought or our slow winter months. You can see some of those letters in the appendix at the back of the book.

Letter #1: You should mail this letter to all your clients you have not worked for in the past twenty-four to thirty-six months. This mailing is to your current clients. You do not need to stick to the direct-mail rules when mailing to past clients. You can use labels, letterhead, and your envelopes. This is a real moneymaker.

I mailed 400 letters and received approximately $20,000 in quick sales. This is incredible and gives us plenty of work to keep busy and also to regroup.

Letter #2: All right, here is another cash-flow surge that you can use. Use this letter to mail to prospects or clients who received bids or proposals, but didn't reward you with the project. This generally brings in approximately $20,000 to $30,000 when we mail it.

Letter #3: This is our "shameless bribe" letter, which is very effective. It is sent to our prospect list. We brought in several thousand dollars with it.

Now, when you look at these letters, there is something you must keep in mind. You have to think outside the box and tweak them to meet what you need in your business.

If you look at letter #2, you will find a compelling headline, a compelling reason to respond. "No payments" until a certain time with "no interest." The subhead is the landscape card, the credit card we offer in our business. You may or may not want to do that.

You go down a little bit and you will find another benefit underlined: "We take all the risk."

On the second page, you will find a very important item that must be in all your letters; it must be in all your marketing material: testimonials.

Your present clients can sing your praises a whole lot better than you can. They are a lot more believable than you or I will ever be when it comes to our own service, so you have to use testimonials.

Later, I will show you some great ways to get testimonials very easily.

Okay, if you go down in the letter, it talks about more referrals. You will see the PS, PPS, and PPPS at the bottom or end of the letter.

It goes back and restates and puts emphasis on the benefits that the client is going to get.

Letter #3 is our "shameless bribe" letter, which brings in new clients.

You want to look it over and see the different things that are involved in it and, here again, think outside of the box. If you need to change things and tweak it for your area or for your services, do it. It has been very effective.

It tells them their savings. It gives them compelling reasons here to use you.

One mistake I made in this letter was that I did not put testimonials inside the letter.

So we sent a list of testimonials on a separate sheet. It's that important.

In the first mailing, this one brought in around $30,000. The second mailing generated around $35,000 to $37,000.

Also, we had this inserted into several newspapers in our area. It brought in about $20,000 to $25,000.

So ... these letters will certainly help you get over the hump in your slow times.

To get these letters and a wealth of other marketing material for your business, go to www.treecaresuccess.com and get FREE information on my "Millionaire Maker" Inner Circle "ELITE" membership.

Strategy 68:
Up-sell and cross-sell

Increase your bottom line immediately: up-sell and cross-sell your clients.

By this, I do not mean bait-and-switch advertising; that is when tell them the low price and then hit them with a much higher price when you get there. By up-selling, I mean offer your clients more ways to help them.

The first up-sell you should go after is fertilizing, a tree-health program with a yearly contract, or an ongoing contract that keeps you feeding and providing treatments until they cancel.

Monthly, quarterly, or biannual programs practically double your profit for not that much more work.

In addition, you can offer a tree-health inspection or monitoring program. This will be a service they value dearly. Make sure to place a price on it so they will appreciate it.

If there are common problems, diseases, or insect infestations with trees in your area, create an inspection specifically for that concern.

Examples would be an oak wilt inspection, or an aphid inspection, etc. This gets you on their property more often. It also cements your relationship with that client.

You can offer a prevention service as an up-sell service. For instance, offer a free health inspection. This service can also be an up-sell. Clients love annual or biannual inspection of their trees and shrubs and are very happy to pay for this annual *renewable*—and that is the key—*automatically renewable* service agreement. Ours is called the Tree Monitor Program.

It gets you on their property up to three times a year, and you will sell a lot of additional services. It also cages that client in. It keeps the client from going to another tree or landscape service.

When they forget about you, you are about to lose a client.

I used to think up-selling was a way to squeeze more money out of a client, and I was wrong. I have seen too much evidence that prevention programs really work and the continuity programs or annual programs are the only way to ensure healthy, safe trees. Those services are a good value to your client. Of course, I do not have to convince you of that.

Okay, how to sell additional services. I learned that most tree or landscape owners hate selling. Do not think of it as selling, think of it as educating. Educate your clients so they can decide for themselves what is best for them. Do not try to spend their money for them. Give them a preponderance of proof, tons and tons of proof. It is always better to have too much than not enough.

Overwhelm them with benefits of using additional tree-care prevention programs. If you do, most will buy them. Do not rely on your crews to sell. Most people hate selling. They are afraid of it. Unless you put in a lot of time and effort to properly train your employee, they will do a very poor job of it and can actually lose you business instead of gain you business.

You can sell many other things besides tree or landscape treatments. Tell your clients about your other services. If you have any other services at all, make sure to tell your clients about them. For example, if you do specific tree work like tree planting or fertilization, tell your client.

You also need to leave them information on how to contact you in case of emergencies. A refrigerator or phone magnet is great for this. That way, if there ever is a need, they can find your number fast. It will also ensure that you get the business, and not your competition.

If you have a service that your client can use right away, make an offer when you are there. Offer them a special deal if they get their tree or landscape work done all at once.

Focus on tree benefits and "what is in it for the client." Make it compelling. Make sure there is a benefit in there for clients. They need a compelling reason to call you—and *only* you—about this service.

Give them the reason why they must call you over any other service or any other way of doing it.

So what else can you sell your clients? Lots and lots of things. However, they should be somewhat related to tree care in most cases:

Offer shrub care or gutter cleaning (around the roof anyway). Also be sure to ask in the survey to your clients what they want from your service.

Section 3: Systems to Make Things Happen

Processes and procedures that keep the marketing machine going

Marketing strategies work when you keep them going. To do that, you need to have systems in place. You also need to be able to measure the results you are getting so that you can test your ideas and make adjustments to improve outcomes.

Set up systems for your marketing programs and educate your employees about them. Make sure that everyone understands how the systems work and that they accommodate the new processes and procedures into their jobs.

Strategy 69:
Discover your "business DNA"

People judge your business by factors that are in most cases invisible to you. How many times have you been turned off by a restaurant simply because of a waiter or waitress's indifference? How many stores do you avoid because of slow service? Are these factors directly related to the quality of the company's product or service? Most often they are not, but they certainly affect the business.

Think about your experiences with businesses in your community, let's say, over the past year. How many left a truly positive experience in your mind? How many were a pain in the neck to do business with? Which ones do you return to?

Ultra-successful businesses become compulsive about seemingly insignificant details. Do you realize there are hundreds, most likely thousands, of details in each facet of your business? Although seemingly unimportant individually, together, they are your business. They are the DNA, the lifeline, lifeblood of your business's existence.

So what is DNA? DNA is the genetic makeup each of us has within every cell of our body. Although we're not conscious of it, it's the very essence of our existence, our genetic fingerprint. Similar elements exist within our businesses. Our business is comprised of many small, seemingly insignificant elements that collectively account for our level of success or failure. So the DNA of your business and my business is every little detail or process inside our business.

Let's go over a few of them now. Let's kind of jog your mind a little bit about what I'm talking about.

In fact, these are things that you can work on in your weekly meetings.

Take them one at a time. I suggest starting with who's answering the phone and how they answer the phone.

We have in our office a recording system set up, voice-activated, tied to our phone lines that we can go and listen to at any time. Our staff knows they are subject to being recorded.

We can go in and listen to how our phone is being answered. We can evaluate how (or whether) our customers are getting their questions answered.

Here's one thing that I want to bring up at this point that may very well surprise you.

How many clients or prospects are you losing on the front end?

Let me give you an example: You do all these marketing things and you take your strategies and they're working and they're getting people to ring your phone.

Do you know what happens when they call? Well, you probably think you do. I thought I did. But how many are not getting their questions answered or how many of them are just thanking them for the information and hanging up? How many are you pre-closing to set up a proposal for or how many are you losing?

It can mean tens of thousands of dollars on your bottom line from clients who call in.

The person either doesn't have the answer to the question, they hem and haw about it, they're too busy, or maybe they do answer the questions, and the client thanks them and goes on.

Well, that's similar to you going and making a proposal. You give the client the proposal, he thanks you, and you just drive off. You don't try to close the sale. You don't try to find out more ways to close the sale. What are the objections? Is it pricing, is it something else?

That's a pre-close. On the phone, your staff needs to do the same type of pre-close. They need to set an appointment for the prospect. They need to bring them into your system. If you're bringing all these prospects into your marketing funnel but you're losing them when they make the call, you need to know that.

You will be amazed at the amount of problems you have on the front end.

I'll just ask a few questions quickly.

Does your receptionist or secretary know how you give proposals? Do they know much about trees? What information do they have in their heads that they can give the client?

Number one, it keeps them from coming to you and taking up your time or your salesmen's time if they know this. So I suggest that you send them through the certified arborist program. They don't have to be certified, but you can send them through it. Teach them what you know about tree and landscape services.

A lot of times, we train our crews, but we forget to train our frontline people who are losing us clients on the front. Shop your phone often.

All right. So let's look at some things that are the DNA of our business.

Number one, how is the phone answered? Is there a phone answering script? It doesn't have to canned, but is there a procedure they go by? What is the procedure for fielding calls? Who fields calls for which particular questions? How can I cut down on general calls that come to my people? How can I streamline the telephone process? How can I make the telephone answering process a positive experience both for my clients and my employees? How can I capture the caller into becoming a client? How can I capture the name and address of each caller from my company mailing list, and how did they learn of us? How did they get hold of us? How can I dramatically separate our phone demeanor from the competition in a powerful and positive way?

So you see what I mean? The simple, seemingly insignificant task of answering the phone is comprised of many hidden elements that you can capitalize on by simply paying attention to the DNA of your business.

You must learn the art of questioning everything. Question every facet of your business. Question what is needed to personalize these seemingly insignificant elements and transform them into a mini representation of your business ideals, your company's personality and attention to detail. Others have built a reputation for the devoted attention to details of their business, and so could you and so could I. We can all do it.

All right. You need to start today. Take a look at everything, no matter how small, no matter how trivial, and ask yourself the following question: "How could I make this small attribute of my business a better representation of my company's overall ideas and identity?"

Reach for the next level.

Remember the following formulas and take your choice as to which you wish to use in your business:

- "Good enough" gets normal results.
- The next level sets new standards.

"Good enough" won't reap big rewards or separate you from the competition. Details can be the deciding factor.

You must escape the sphere of mediocrity and give your business, as well as the services it offers, the attention that will springboard it ahead of the competition. You can do this just by understanding and focusing on its DNA.

Strategy 70:
Create a marketing system

A marketing system is a system used to get leads. We talked earlier about a marketing plan. In this marketing plan, you need to build a system.

Actually, all of the strategies in this book are systems.

Yes, they are strategic ways of getting new clients, but they are systems. You cannot just do part of one and expect to get results. It just does not happen that way. You will get results, but you will have to do every part of the system, not just the first step. This is true of any system.

Think about making coffee. The first step is to put in a new filter and then add the coffee, but if you stop there, you will never get coffee. You need to follow the rest of the steps in the system to get the coffee. That is, you have to add water. The second step is to put the pot under the drip, and turn it on. Then you will have coffee.

Stopping at the first few steps in any marketing strategy will give you the same results as with your coffeemaker and that is simply none. So, follow through on everything, complete the system, and you will soon be making thousands of dollars more a month than you ever have before.

Strategy 71:
Keep a client database

It's very important that you create some sort of client database to capture all phone numbers and pertinent information on your clients. It can be something as simple as a flat-file database that just captures name and address. But if at all possible, you want a database that captures more information, such as their source, where they heard of you, why they called you, etc.

You also, if possible, want to capture their birthdays and more information about their property. But the main thing is to capture the names, phone numbers, and addresses of all your clients. This will enable you to get marketing material out to them very quickly.

Then, later, you will build this database up more as you begin to use these strategies.

If you just have them on a piece of paper, it's a lot tougher to get things out quickly. When you need to use different things such as mail merge, it makes it much simpler for you to correspond with your clients.

You have to develop your electronic (computer) database as soon as possible. It is the biggest goldmine or asset you own.

You could lose everything you have, but if you have your client list, you can be back in business tomorrow, especially using these strategies.

If you don't have them in a database, I highly suggest you take the time. Put in so many names daily or weekly until you get them in there.

That way you can market to them very quickly.

Strategy 72:
Create a sales system

Systemize your sales calls and your sales procedure.

When you get something that works, write it out, and require it to be adhered to by your sales personnel or your sales arborists.

If you look at our marketing materials, you can see the sales process that we have available.

It's just simply a process that they go through before they leave the office in the mornings and they go through with each client.

You must have a sales script for consistent sales and profits.

It's very effective.

Strategy 73:
Keep a networking file

Once you set up a database for your clients, you also want to set up a network database file. This is simply a network of businesses that will refer you. We call it our network file.

This one simple thing has been very, very successful for our company and others.

What is a network file?

It is anybody you can think of in your service area who would get the question asked to them "Do you know someone who does tree or landscape services (or whatever service you offer)?"

Say you do tree care, but you don't do lawn and landscape services. You want people who do provide these services in your network file. If you are a lawn service or landscape service, you don't do tree service, then you're going to want tree services in your network file. Other examples are irrigation companies, roofing companies, painting companies, and remodeling companies.

One great network type that just continues to send us business is hardware stores and lumber stores. Another great one is nurseries. We get a lot of referrals from nurseries. You want to make certain that you have them on your mailing list.

So every time you send a marketing piece out, especially your newsletter (you have a newsletter, don't you?), they get all this material.

So what happens is—it works tremendously in my business—you'll get a lot of referrals from companies you've never worked for. The reason? They're constantly seeing your name and information in front of them, so if they do not have a personal relationship with another tree or landscape firm, then they will immediately refer you to the client that they're doing work for. That is a great way to get referrals.

You'll see a tremendous bump in your business once you do this. In fact, I have given this to consulting clients of mine before and it immediately began to get results for them.

Strategy 74:
Create a new-client or prospect kit

A new-client or prospect kit is a packet of information you send to every new client. This package includes your thank-you letter, information about your other services, any of your client programs, your referral programs, and of course, some past newsletters.

This new-client or prospect kit does many things for you. It reinforces that your company is extraordinary. It makes your client think that he or she is getting a lot more than just a tree or landscape job. It enables you to get more referrals. It encourages your client or prospect to use your other services.

Here are examples of what to include in your new-client kit:

1. A thank-you letter or card.
2. Your referral program information.
3. Current and past newsletters.
4. Information and an offer on other services.

A new-client or prospect kit is a cheap, easy way to get more business from each client and to get referrals. This is definitely a moneymaker.

Here is another thing a new-client or prospect kit will do for you and your profits. It's called "pre-emptive selling." If you get it to the prospect or client before your competition, it will put in their mind what to bring up and ask the competition. Do they guarantee their work in writing? Do they use industry-accepted pruning standards? Do they carry full required insurance? Etc., etc., etc.

If you have a Web site, all the information in the new-client or prospect kit needs to be on it. When they call you and you cannot get it to them soon enough, send them to your Web site to review you and your company.

And so, this is a way to get a leg up in the selling process and also to up your profits.

Strategy 75:
Set up your voicemail to market for you

Voicemail is a way you can save valuable time and sell more.

Let's go over that.

Voicemail is getting to be everywhere, so you have got to learn how to manipulate it and do it right. Every day, you repeat the same information over and over to prospects about how they should get their trees pruned and inspected regularly—and the consequences if they don't. If you count every minute you spent with prospects or clients, selling them something, it would probably add up to two to four hours. That is two to four hours every single day.

Realize that 90 percent of this information was the same for everybody.

This is how you can save an average of approximately two hours every day.

Create a voicemail message. You will notice a lot of companies are doing this now. It will cover why your tree or landscape method is best, how to choose a good tree or landscape company, why a certified arborist is best, all the things you use to sell your company. Call it as we do, our "consumer awareness message." Anyone can call it twenty-four hours a day, and hear valuable information.

The voicemail message is non-threatening. When someone calls it, they know they don't have to talk to anyone. They don't have to be afraid of being pressured into anything. It is risk-free. It is a recorded message, so anyone who is even slightly interested will call.

Plus, it qualifies prospects for you. Would you rather talk to twenty really interested prospects—or one hundred suspects? Out of the one hundred, only twenty are interested, but you have to talk to all of them to figure out which ones.

That is a tremendous waste of time. Wouldn't you much rather spend your time with qualified, interested leads? It is much more productive.

So the voicemail screens out the bad leads. You can use the voicemail for all sorts of things. Explain all your different services. It is cheap, plus it is a selling tool that sells twenty-four hours a day, seven days a week. No secretaries or answering services are needed. You can't beat that. It also eliminates those bad days. You just have to do the voicemail well once, and then use it forever. There aren't any bad days.

This has worked very well in our company. There is no reason why it won't work in your tree or landscape company also.

If you would like the phone number of a very good voicemail company, just give me or my office a call or you can hire a local one. If you would like to talk to me about it, shoot me an e-mail at john@treecaresuccess.com.

Call ours, listen to it, see what you think. It is a very good tool.

Why do it alone? Go to www.treecaresuccess.com and sign up for a membership in my "Millionaire Maker" Inner Circle Program.

Strategy 76:
Have a system for follow-up calls

As you've done business with people, you'll find follow-up is very seldom done. This is by far the most neglected item in a selling or customer service system.

Follow-up calls are made one to three days after you service someone's trees or their landscape. Have someone in your office call and check up on the satisfaction of the client. It's much, much more effective when the person who sold the job does the follow-up.

This strategy is very effective. The number-one reason businesses lose clients is because a client doesn't feel wanted. They think the business doesn't care about them. Sure, some clients leave because they move or they die, but many more leave because they're unhappy or they don't feel too important. Of these two, the latter is by far the larger.

Follow-up calls don't take much time to make sure your client's happy. I've seen many clients who weren't happy over something very minor become happy clients because of the follow-up call. It's much cheaper to keep an existing client happy than it is to get a new client. That's why client service is so important. And because it's more and more difficult to catch people at home, here's a sequence to take for follow-up calls:

1. Call in the afternoon.
2. If no answer, call in the evening.
3. If still no answer, leave a message.
4. Also send a card if you left a message.

This strategy can recover a lot of business that otherwise would have been lost. It also makes people happy to see that you really care, and they'll be more likely to refer you to others. So it's very important that you make follow-up calls.

Because other companies aren't doing it, it will cause you to stand out and cement the relationship with your client.

Strategy 77:
Conduct target farming

Target farming is niche marketing. Niche marketing is targeting a specific group, like certain neighborhoods or certain professions such as doctors or small-business owners. The group has something in common with each other. It is much easier to target certain niches than it is to target everyone. You will get much greater response.

People feel important if you specialize in them. This is very true. Think about it. Which would you be more likely to use—a generic insurance agent or one who specializes in insuring tree or landscape companies? Would you have bought this program if it were just a generic marketing program for training and business? Probably not. Specializing is good.

Pick two to three niche markets that you would like to get into. It could be a wealthy neighborhood; it could be lawyers; it could be doctors, country club members, golfers, or Mercedes owners. The options are unlimited. Pick two to three and start really targeting them. For instance, a particular affluent neighborhood:

1. Put them on your newsletter mailing list.
2. Mail a sales letter.
3. Put out door hangers when the crew is in the area.
4. Then do a voucher pack or money mailer type ad that goes to that neighborhood.

We do this in neighborhoods we want to build up. Call it your prospect list. It is highly, highly successful.

Once you get a few of them, then start using testimonials from them. You can dominate this niche in a very short time by doing this.

Then pick up another niche market and do the same thing.

You can specialize in a million different niches. Being the tree or landscape company for doctors doesn't stop you from being the tree or landscape company for printers also.

A good way to get into a professional niche is with a champion letter.

All right, let's say you want to target doctors. You have one doctor as a client. This doctor really likes you. She thinks you are the greatest tree or landscape expert on Earth, so you go to her and you ask her if she is willing to endorse you. Don't worry, she will, in most all cases.

Here's how you do it. You write a letter from her to all the other doctors in your area. This letter should tell how wonderful she thinks you are and it should include the message, "We doctors are so busy, I don't have any spare time to waste," and then she tells them about you so they don't waste their time with any of the unprofessional tree or landscape companies. Also enclose a sales letter of your own, offering a free tree health care evaluation.

Send this letter from the doctor on her letterhead and her envelopes. Also stapled to her letter is her business card. Pay for all the letterhead, envelopes, and business cards and, of course, the postage. Then give the doctor extra business cards or letterhead as a thank-you.

What this will do is ensure that your letter gets opened and read. All doctors read mail from other doctors, just like if you received a letter from another tree or landscape company, you are generally going to read it. You are curious as to why another tree company is writing.

Don't forget to follow up with a second and third letter with your current or past newsletters from just you, not the doctor. Be sure to do that.

This type of niche marketing is very powerful.

It is also a lot easier to get referrals when you niche market.

All your clients know others in their same niche, and they think you specialize in their niche and in their profession. They know others will want to use you, too.

It is a very, very powerful way to target an area and become the tree company of choice.

Strategy 78:
Get and use testimonials

Testimonials are what your current clients have to say about you. Testimonials are very important. What others say about you is infinitely more believable than what you say about you.

Think about it: Would you be more likely to try a new restaurant if your neighbor told you how wonderful it is or if you saw an ad in the newspaper for it? Of course, you'd more likely try it if your neighbor couldn't stop bragging about it. That's another marketing strategy: Make people so thrilled with your service that they can't help telling others about you.

Look back at our "Wow Your Client" strategy. Testimonials add credibility and make your company seem more believable.

How many testimonials should you use? You can never have too many testimonials. Sure, maybe your prospects won't read every one, but they'll read enough to be convinced. They'll assume that others are just as good.

To show you the power of testimonials, let me tell you about a public speaker. As you may know, public speaking is a tough business. There are lots and lots of speakers out there—there's fierce competition.

One public speaker doesn't write any letters or any marketing materials to send a prospect. This is all he does: When someone calls his office and asks for information about a speaking engagement, he gets their name and address. Then he sends them a box—a big box, full of what past clients have had to say. That's all he does. No letter, nothing else. He closes 82 percent of all his prospects and is fully booked.

Testimonials are truly very powerful. Use as many testimonials as you can, because they make the difference between a marketing strategy working and not working. They make the difference between you closing the sale and not closing the sale, because remember, we talked about it before—people who hire tree or landscape services don't really trust them. Especially if they don't know who they're hiring. They don't really understand and so you're not in their comfort zone.

It's much more powerful if you can get testimonials from people in prospects' neighborhoods. That works like gangbusters and will actually sell for you. So you want to be sure and do that.

Strategy 79: How to get testimonials

We've already talked about a couple. What if you don't have any testimonials? Well, that's okay. You can get them pretty quickly.

First, talk to your clients, the ones you know, and the ones who think highly of you, and who really love your service. The ones who think you are the best thing since sliced bread. Ask them for testimonials, but don't leave it up to them to write them from scratch. Most people don't like to write, and second of all, they don't write in an emotionally compelling style. Make it easy for them. Give them a sheet of questions to answer and make sure it is okay to use them as testimonials in your marketing materials.

Then turn those answers into sentences. Make them compelling. Don't forget to get their permission to use their name; otherwise, you can get yourself in trouble.

I like to offer them a box to check if they aren't willing to let me use their name in promotional material.

Start taking the form to every job. Ask every client to please take a few minutes and fill it out. Then after they've seen the results of the job and when the crew is finished picking up, have them look over it and sign it. Most clients will be more than happy to do this for you.

Just because you don't have testimonials, don't put off doing something. Do it. You can always add testimonials, but if you have them and use them.

Strategy 80:
What testimonials should say

Another rule of thumb for testimonials is to have at least one testimonial for each benefit. For example, if one of your benefits is a charming personality, then have one testimonial that says how great you are when you come to the home.

For every benefit, you should have at least one testimonial. Two is better. You can't have too many testimonials. The purpose of testimonials is to create credibility so prospects believe that what you're saying about yourself is true. The best way to do that is to give the person's name and occupation, and city and state, if you've got it. For example: "James Brady, nurse, Aurora, Colorado."

Don't worry if some of your testimonials are stay-at-home moms or stay-at-home dads or spouses. That's fine, because if a good portion of your clients are stay-at-home moms, then you'll want to attract more stay-at-home moms. This only becomes a problem when you're trying to sell something to janitors and all your testimonials are from upper-management employees. The testimonials should be similar to your actual prospect, and again, if you can get it in their area, then that works much, much better.

Strategy 81:
Keep a book of testimonials

Keep a record of testimonials. Every time you get a testimonial, put it in your book of testimonials. This can be a three-ring notebook or a nice leather-bound one. It doesn't matter, as long as you have one.

You should take this testimonial book or list of testimonials to every tree or landscape quote that you do.

Let your prospects look at it.

If you have the book, let them look through it. Encourage them to look at it. When a prospect sees how many clients are thrilled with your services, he will also want to do business with you.

What other people say about you is more believable than what you say about you. Your prospect may even recognize some of your clients' names. He may know them as neighbors, friends, and may even have association from work, etc.

This is very, very powerful.

Having all of these testimonials is equivalent to lots and lots of referrals saying how wonderful you are and how wonderful your company is. This is very easy to do, and you'll get tremendous results from it. So if you haven't started that, you need to get that going ASAP.

Strategy 82:
Set up a referral program

Referrals are the fastest, easiest way to double your business, bar none.

What if you could get all your current clients to refer just one person this year?

Would that be really difficult?

NO! But what a difference it would make to your bottom line.

You may think that it's impossible if you rarely get a referral now. But believe me, it's not difficult.

However, you have to make it happen. It won't happen by itself. You should aim all your efforts at getting referrals. Why? Referred clients, like I said before, are simply better and more profitable clients.

1. They cost less to acquire. This is very important. Anything you can do to get your cost-per-client down is great.
2. They are much less price-resistant, because they were referred by someone they trust; they really want your service.
3. They are more likely to refer, since they were referred by someone else.
4. They are less likely to complain and are easy to please. Even if something does go wrong, referred clients are much more understanding. On the whole, they're simply much easier to please.

For all these reasons, you should make getting referrals your number-one priority. This won't just happen. Like anything else, you have to make it happen. Don't let any opportunity pass you by to ask for a referral. When a client calls in to say what a wonderful job you did, thank them, and ask for a referral. It's easy, and you'll get results.

To maximize your referrals, you must have a referral program in place. It can be the reward program or recognition program, but you simply must use one of them. Use one of them and get going. It's simply free money.

Strategy 83:
Reward your referrers

Recognize every client and company that refers you. Ask every prospect who is referred to you if you may please have the name of the client who referred them so you can thank them and send them a small gift.

Send them a "We Love Referrals" card, or maybe some $20 "Tree Bucks." This is absolutely powerful and hardly costs anything. They can give these to neighbors, friends, and relatives—doesn't matter who.

Let them accumulate them if they like.

Of course, if you gave cold, hard cash, I certainly believe that would work much better.

But do this, because it works.

Clients are not looking for a big, expensive gift. They just want recognition, and you'll be rewarded very well also.

Strategy 84:
Establish a monetary reward referral program

This reward referral program is based on monetary compensation or giving away gifts. Number one is money. The monetary system is an easy way to develop a referral program quickly.

For every referral who becomes a client, you pay the client who referred you $10 or $20. You can write a check and drop it off, or you can send it in the mail.

To help generate more than one referral from each client, you can have an increasing value for each referral. For instance, for referrals one to three, you pay $10. But on referral four, you pay $20. I like this because it rewards clients who refer more people and gives them more money.

Another way is to pay $10 for referrals one through three, and then $20 for referral four—and just start all over again. So referral five is equal to referral one. You can get amazing results from this. Rewards that are cash tend to do better than those that only offer money off of the next purchase. You'll find this out.

The other type of reward referral program is based on giving away items of value, instead of money. You can offer free movie tickets, free facials, free massages, a free month at the gym, free manicure, etc. The list is just endless. Give your clients a choice, and list three different things they can win if one of their referrals becomes a client.

If you up the ante for more than one referral, you'll get more referrals per client. For instance, you can have a choice of three things for one referral, five things for two referrals, seven things for three referrals, etc. Each category should have increasing values of clients. If you choose deals that your clients really want, you'll get better results with gifts than with money. But on the other hand, if you don't know what your clients really want, stick with money. Either way, make sure you recognize your clients who referred you new clients in your newsletter. Make sure they get recognition. Let me tell you something: Clients love recognition, and like I said awhile ago, they will certainly reward you back in return. We've proven that time and time again.

Strategy 85:
Track referral sources

You should know where every client comes from BEFORE your initial appointment. This is to confirm that the new client actually came from the same source that you thought.

Plus, it gives you an easy way to get referrals right off the bat. All your clients should feel that giving you referrals is natural and expected of them. If they feel this way and you ask them frequently, you'll get tons of referrals.

Here is an example of a form to have your first-time client fill out after you finished the job:

Tracking/Referral Form

Name:_____

I heard about you from the following:

A. I am a previous client_____
B. Saw the ad in the newspaper____
C. Was referred by a friend_____ Name of friend_____
D. Saw the ad in the Yellow Pages____
E. Received a letter_____
F. Other_____

Strategy 86:
Track your results

Why must you track your results? If you do not know what is working and what is not, you will have no way to increase your business. Things are not always as they seem. You cannot guess whether something is working or not. You must keep track of the numbers and let them tell you.

Let me give you a few examples:

> Ad A costs $350 to run. It goes to 10,000 prospects. You get twelve clients from it.
>
> Ad B is a direct-mail piece. It costs $400 to send it to 200 prospects. You get four new clients. Which is better?

At first it may seem that A is better, but let's look at the rest of the numbers. Ad A: The twelve clients generated had an average job of $200. Two of them had you go back out and redo trees they were not happy with; eleven out of the twelve complained that your prices were too high.

All right, now let's look at Ad B. The four clients generated had an average job of $900; none of them complained about the price; one of them referred two clients to you while you were doing the job.

So you made $2,400 off the front end of Ad A. A cost you $350; that is $2,050 left. The back end is not very big, because there were no referrals.

Ad B, on the other hand, generated $3,600 on the front end. The back end is even bigger because of the referrals. The cost of Ad B was $400 so that is $3,200 left, not including referral revenue—which is more than Ad A generated all together.

I hope now you can see why you must keep track of the numbers. Some methods may be misleading when you think you are doing great but you really aren't. Don't have an idea whether something is working well? Know your numbers and then you will know for sure.

Strategy 87:
Track clients and prospects

Repeat client? Referral? Referral from whom? Yellow Pages ad? Phone number off trucks?

Where do your clients come from? You have to know these statistics. If you don't know, you are running blind and probably wasting lots of money. You or your secretary should ask every prospect, "May I ask where you heard of our services?" up front. They will be happy to tell you.

Track where your clients and prospects come from, and you will be amazed at the results and the savings in your advertising bill.

Strategy 88:
Know your numbers

This is crucial to making you tons of money. If you don't know your numbers, you have no idea what's working and what's not. If you don't know what's working, you can't possibly do more of what it is that's working. You can't just have a good idea—you need to know for sure.

Many tree or landscape companies have been wrong about what is working and what isn't working. They think something's working, but it turns out that it's barely breaking even. Or they think it's failing and they stop doing it, when in reality it was actually doing five-to-one against the odds, which is great. You need to know the following to calculate your numbers:

1. The cost of the ad or the mailing.
2. The number of leads generated from it.
3. How many of the leads turned into clients.
4. The average dollar amount per client.
5. The average number of referrals per client.

Once you calculate these numbers, you compare them to your average numbers. That way, you can see which methods are working better for you. This is the only way to get ahead. Know your numbers or let me tell you, advertising simply ain't worth doing.

Strategy 89:
Hold weekly meetings

You must have weekly meetings to keep on track. It doesn't matter if you have lots of employees or you're by yourself; you still have to have weekly meetings. The purpose of these meetings is to see how you're doing, to see how close you are to your goals. After you see how you're doing, you need to plan for the next week.

Schedule an hour a week for this meeting. We schedule two hours here at this office. It has to be at the same time every week, such as Tuesdays from 8:00 to 10:00 AM, or 10:00 AM to noon—no exceptions. Do not schedule bids or proposals during the time you plan for the meeting.

Don't make the mistake of thinking you will do the meeting some other time—it won't happen. Pick a time, stick with it, once a week, no less often, and no more often. These weekly meetings will help you implement more strategies and do more of the ones that are making you tons of money. This isn't difficult. You just have to make a commitment and stick to it.

During the meeting, list your priorities and strategies. Write down the steps that need to be accomplished in order to carry out each strategy. Mark off the list as you accomplish each step until that strategy is done. It's very difficult to succeed without having weekly meetings and a list of objectives. What you do to accomplish a strategy is what keeps you on course, week in and week out. If you've got employees or staff in your office, weekly meetings are important to keep people up to date on where you're at, and to keep them focused on moving ahead.

Another main reason for weekly meetings is to go over accounts receivable and any complaints to make sure they are resolved in a timely manner.

We handle any problems with clients and any other issues we need to get out of the way at the first of the meeting. Then we go over the different strategies that we're putting in force. We go around the table, find out where we're at on them and how we're doing.

It works very well. It keeps you more relaxed, because unless it's an emergency, people bring their concerns and interests to that meeting. Then you're not handling issues all the time. You bring them to that meeting and discuss them there.

If you want to go over something with some of your staff, you write it down. I keep a meeting note manual, and write down anything I need to bring up during that meeting, so I can make sure that I get it taken care of.

Strategy 90:
Test. And test. And test.

Always, always test your marketing methods on a small scale. Then if they work—and only if they work—test a little bigger. Keep getting bigger and bigger if it works. I have known many people to lose their shirts by not following this rule. In fact, one of those people was me.

No matter how wonderful you think your idea or plan is, test small. Let the response tell you if it is good or not. Let the market tell you. If you buy 500 names from a mailing-list broker, mail to 500 names and if you get a tremendous response, then you do a bigger mailing. You decide to mail the rest of the list, which is 12,500 names. You spend $12,500 to buy the list (at $1 a name) and spend $5,125 on postage (when stamps are 41 cents each). You have to SELL approximately 30 jobs with an average of $600 to break even.

Probably tough to do.

So watch out, you could loose your rear.

Mailing brokers always give you the best part of the list first. The most responsive buyers. In this example, with no sales you've lost $17,625. This is a common mistake. Many, many people have made it.

Remember, test, test, test.

Test small, get bigger slower.

Always test small.

Section 4: Growing the Business

Strategies to add in once you're really moving

I've given you a lot of things to put into place for marketing success. It's going to take time for you to get everything up and running, but it will be so worth it!

You will master it. You will have all the systems in place, and your staff will be following all the processes and procedures like clockwork. You will be generating more leads than ever, and your client base will grow.

You can't stop. One of the true things about business is that you are either growing or deteriorating; there is no such thing as treading water or "arriving." If you stop pushing, your competition will take business away from you, you will miss changes in the marketplace, and you will lose opportunities because you aren't paying attention.

So, once you have your systems in place, keep growing. This section covers some ways to do just that.

Strategy 91:
Raise your prices

Do not be afraid. Everyone wants to raise their prices, but they are afraid to. A person only buys on price when they think all other aspects are equal or nearly equal.

What I mean by this is that no one would buy a Mercedes if they thought the only difference between a Yugo and a Mercedes was the price. To overcome price shopping, you have to educate your prospects so they realize what they are getting.

For most people, one tree or landscape company is no different from the next tree or landscape company.

They think we are all the same.

They think every method is the same, and every company does the same thing.

That is why they price shop.

Why would anyone want to pay more for the same thing? Your job is to convince them that all tree or landscape services are not the same.

You know this; you just have to convince them. Once you do this, your worries are over concerning pricing.

Don't wait for your client to say that you are expensive or out of their budget. It is almost always too late at that point. You should educate them right from the beginning. Your clients are not accustomed to buying the cheapest products. They live in nice houses, they have nice cars, and they wear nice clothes.

Why?

Because they know the difference between price and value. You just have to make them look at products or services the same way that they look at other things. This is easy when your clients are middle class and above.

Raise your prices.

Get paid for what you do.

You deserve it.

Strategy 92:
Add more services

Adding more services is a way to increase your profits.

There are some downsides to each of them. If you offer lawn services, for instance, you have to buy more equipment. All of them have their pros and cons. Think about this before you expand.

Other services can be profitable, and you can piggyback them to your current services. Additional services do not have to be advertised to the general public to get new clients. Of course you can advertise them, but it's easier to live on the clients you get from your existing service company.

This means that extra services get clients without expensive advertising. That's why this can be very profitable. An excellent add-on is home and landscape pest control. Most tree or landscape services already have a certified or licensed technician on the payroll.

We added this service. At the time, it was an estimated addition of approximately $75,000 to our gross sales the very first year. This service was offered to our tree-care clients almost exclusively.

So, you want to look at things that can add revenue and profit, but do not add to your advertising budget.

Strategy 93:
Diversify your market

Diversity equals stability.

If you have one marketing strategy that is pulling in $20,000 a month, which is entirely possible, it can be tempting not to do anything else. This is a mistake. This makes you very vulnerable. It's like putting all your eggs in one basket. If, for some reason, that strategy starts only pulling in half as much—only $10,000—you're in trouble.

I know, I know. I keep telling you these strategies are systems and that they get consistent results. This is all true, but there can always be some sort of change in one's system. Over time, things are bound to happen. If you have ten different strategies to get new clients each month, that's better than one.

The more reliable systems you have bringing in a steady flow of new clients, the more stable you will be.

For example, if you have ten different strategies bringing in $10,000 a month, and one stops working, you'll still be fine. But if you only have one, and it stops working, let me tell you, you've got big trouble.

I'm telling you this because individual strategies are extremely powerful. One strategy could easily bring in $20,000 or more a month. It'll be tempting just to do that one, but don't. Diversify. Your company will be bigger, better, and certainly more stable.

Why do it alone? I've got dozens of low- to no-cost strategies to increase your sales quickly! **Go to www.treecaresuccess.com and sign up for membership in my "Millionaire Maker" Inner Circle Program.**

Strategy 94:
Network

Do it right or don't do it.

What I mean is that some people are better at networking than others. When they go to meetings, parties, etc., they interact. They talk to strangers and get to know them. They make contacts and maybe the contacts become clients.

Others go to these same meetings and only talk to people they already know. They don't interact with strangers. They are shy, timid— whatever you want to call it.

If you are in group one, then network all you can. If you are in group two, then don't.

Don't feel bad about it; that is just the way you are.

Don't fight it.

Don't waste your time trying to network.

Can someone learn to network? Of course, but it takes work. And frankly, with all these great strategies you now have, you don't need to network.

Learning how to network takes time and effort. The rewards are great. You can get a lot of business by networking but it takes a lot of effort.

Strategy 95:
Launch a charity program

There are many things you can do with charities to generate business. However—take this to heart—only do them if you're truly interested in helping the charity.

Do not do this solely to get new business. If you do, it's probably going to backfire on you. We give consistently to organizations that help people. We don't do it to get business from them. In fact, with some of them, there's no way to get business from them. They give to the poor among us. So we donate to different food banks.

I think it's a good thing to do. It makes you feel good.

We don't advertise it—we just do it.

I'm a firm believer that if you want to get what you want, you're going to have to help other people get what they want. But you don't do it for that reason. You do it because it's simply just a good thing to do, as a good citizen. So, having said that, let's go on.

If you try to help a charity that's not interesting to you and it's just for business, it's probably just going to backfire on you. People are very cautious of others who want to use a charity to help their own business out, so this will be detected, and it'll ruin your whole program.

Only do it if you're sincere.

So if you really want to do a charity program, okay. There are many different things you can do for the charity, including workshops, events, and promotions.

You can do a regular workshop, but with a charity. All the same concepts apply. The only difference is the organization is a charity. You can do an event—you can sponsor a charity event. And it doesn't have to cost you much either. For example, you sponsor a golf tournament with proceeds going to the charity. You could charge each golfer around $50 to $100 to be at the event. You get the charity to promote it.

Be sure you write the actual ads, letters, and announcements, based on our most direct response rules. Then you can get other local merchants to buy advertising during the golf event.

You put up boards and advertisements on each hole or on every other hole. You may make some money on this, but you'll probably just break even.

Your profits will come from getting new clients. Make sure there is plenty of media coverage—newspapers, TV, radio, etc. Since the proceeds go to the charity, the media won't mind publicizing the phone number for more information.

This is another way you can get the golfers. In a short period, your business will get a lot of recognition. This is super, since it shouldn't cost you much. You could even make money on it. Get every golfer's name and address. Send them a letter in the mail, thanking them for golfing, telling them how much you and the golfers raised for the charity, and more importantly, offer them a free tree-care evaluation or free evaluation for trees or landscape.

You can also send a letter to every person who is part of the charity. The charity will have a list that you can mail to. You tell them how you sponsored the golf tournament, how much you raised for the charity, and what the charity is going to do with the money. Then you tell them you're going to help them out since they've helped out the charity also. Offer them a free tree-care evaluation or free landscape evaluation, and a discount if they use your services.

To do a charity event is a lot of work, but you'll make money for the charity and for your business.

Number three is a promotion. A promotion is sending out sales letters to all charity members or donors; of course, you use a three-letter sequence. You have to call the charity and find the person in charge of promotions. Meet with him, and explain that you want to send a letter to all the charity members, offering them a free tree-care evaluation or a free landscape evaluation. Tell him that you will donate a certain percentage of all the work you get from the members, plus you offer the members a discount.

Sometimes you can convince the charity to pay for the postage. Sometimes the charity will split it with you. And once in a while, the charity will insist that you pay for all the postage. If they do, you take that amount out of the amount being donated to the charity.

Make sure the letters go on the charity's letterhead and envelopes—this is very important. It helps to get the coordinator to write a cover letter also endorsing your company.

So you can even offer care for the trees at the charity offices for free. This is a very good strategy that definitely helps. That way, the charity is confident in your work, and they get something out of it right away.

Strategy 96: Target Realtors

Realtors can be the key to many jobs from one client.

Realtors work with both the buyers and the sellers. You can bet at some point in the transaction, the house needs some sort of tree or landscape service.

If you live in an area that has major storm or disease problems, develop a closer relationship with the Realtors. Often the Realtors suggest to the seller that he should have a tree root inspection. In some areas, this isn't the case. Sometimes it's only during the close that the tree inspection is called for.

What the Realtor usually doesn't tell the client is to have his trees pruned or fertilized. By putting the Realtor in a perfect position to recommend a good tree or landscape company, you create an incredible ally. If the seller doesn't get the trees cared for, then usually the buyer will.

So the Realtor's in a great position to recommend a tree or landscape service—and that's you—to the buyer. The best thing about Realtors is that once you get one to recommend you, they'll give you many, many jobs.

You won't have to wait three to twelve months to get a repeat job. A good Realtor should give you at least two jobs a month. If you get ten or twenty Realtors recommending you, that's twenty to forty extra jobs a month. That can be a tremendously profitable thing for you.

Okay, so how do you get Realtors to recommend you?

Your first Realtor is the hardest. Once you get one, getting others is much easier. Realtors hang out with other

Realtors, so once you get one who's happy with you, you can get him to help you to get other Realtors. If you know a Realtor, start with him. If you don't, you can still get into this niche. Most Realtors work for a broker, like Century 21 or ReMax. All of these brokers have weekly meetings. Usually they have someone come in and give a talk for ten or fifteen minutes.

The Realtor who is in charge of these meetings has a very, very difficult time getting enough speakers. It's very easy to get to speak at one of these meetings. Contact the company and ask to speak to the person in charge of the weekly sales meetings for the Realtors. Call this person and tell him who you are, what you want to do, and ask when he can fit you in. These people are usually desperate. You will be an angel to them. They should schedule you in three to four weeks.

When you speak to the Realtors, you need to do several different things:

1. Explain that Realtors are in a perfect position to recommend a tree or landscape company, since the buyer usually gets their trees cared for anyway.
2. Explain that you are a very good tree or landscape company. Use your USP.

Give the Realtors a reason to use you. You can give them $10 for every job, or a certain percentage, or you can say, after they've given you so many jobs, you'll trim or fertilize their trees for free. Whatever you choose, make it crystal clear what they get. Sometimes it's good to put it in writing.

For example, if you give 5 percent of every job, then tell them how much your average job is, and then tell them how much they'd make from referring you for an average job.

You should have at least thirty Realtors at this meeting.

Follow up by sending them a letter, re-explaining your offer and you can expect to get one or two Realtors who continually recommend your services. These one or two gems will refer a lot of business to you. Explain to them exactly what a referral is.

It is not just saying, "Oh, by the way, Mr. and Mrs. Jones, if you get your trees pruned, use ABC Company." This leads to too much chance. So go into detail on how to do a referral and what a referral is, and it will be much more successful.

Strategy 97:
Increase business from Realtor referrals

After a Realtor has given you a referral and you care for their trees, you are in a perfect position to get another client. Whether the buyers of the house hired you or not, you should get them as new clients. They've seen your work and they know you're good.

If the buyer was the one who hired you, then it's easy. Convert him to a repeat client. This is just the same as any other first-time client.

But if the seller hires you, you can still get another new client or two. First of all, lots of times, the sellers are moving, but not very far. If this is the case, you can get the seller to get the trees trimmed at his new house, and turn him into a regular client. If the sellers move out of town, you can't do it. Don't worry about it—you can still get the buyer.

Even though the buyer did not actually hire you, you can send him a letter, of course. Tell him that you are the one who pruned his trees. You've already worked with them. They know your work. This puts you in a great position to get them as clients.

Also, don't forget that the Realtor has a home also!

Strategy 98:
Add services without adding work

Wouldn't it be nice to make money on work you didn't even do? You bet. Well, you can.

For instance, if you don't do gutter cleaning, but one of your clients wants her gutters cleaned, you still make money. You can sub it out to someone who does gutters. You pay them, she pays you, and you keep the difference. Or you can just refer her to another company and earn a referral fee. Check to make sure that's legal in your area before you do it.

When you decide on the services, begin to promote all the services that you offer. For instance, tree-care services, lot maintenance, gutter cleaning, drive and curb cleaning, or lighting-installation services. There are a lot of things that you can add on.

You can offer all these things, and actually only do tree or landscape services. What you have to do is find a company that does one of the other services you offer. Make sure that company does a good job and is also polite to your clients. So you can either collect a referral fee or something else from them.

If you choose to collect a referral fee, you're certainly going to have to stay on top of the other business.

Have them send you a weekly report of all the clients they received from you. You should send them a list of all the clients you referred, and then they report which ones they did work for.

Stay on top of this, or you'll be ripped off.

Remember: If you do this, you'll still have to take responsibility for the other company's work. It's your client—you want to make them happy.

If you refer a bad company, the client's certainly going to hold you responsible, and so they should.

Take responsibility.

Offer a guarantee, even if the other company doesn't.

This is the way to make extra profit for little or no work, but you have to do it right. It may take some time to find good companies, but it's certainly worth the effort.

We offer a guarantee, and we require the other company to do so too.

We do this with our tree-planting and other services. We require they offer a good guarantee to us before we give them the business.

Why?

It just makes sense.

You may have to convince them of that, which is not that hard to do.

Strategy 99:
Speed up the slow season

Every business says they have a slow season.

That may be true—if you let it happen. In the Fort Worth/Dallas area, where I have my companies, the slow season is the winter. For ten years, I had a slow season in the winter.

I believed it.

I didn't think I had a choice.

I was wrong.

I hated the slow season.

Just because it was wet and cold didn't mean I didn't like to make money, so I started brainstorming. I found ways to overcome the slow season.

The first thing is to start planning months before your slow season starts—this is critical. You have to start doing things before you're in the middle of the slow time.

Why?

If you wait until you're in the peak of the slow season, you've already wasted a lot of time.

Plus, all of the strategies you need to use to overcome the slow season take a bit of time. Nothing is instant.

So start by planning a few months before. I realize that this will probably be in your busy season. That means that you have to take the time to plan during your busy season. Believe me, it's worth it.

I've seen too many people who were too busy to plan. Next thing you know, you have more than enough time to plan, and then you're in big trouble. So always, always plan ahead.

You're going to have to beef up your regular marketing and advertising. This will help compensate for your slow season.

Double whatever marketing or advertising method is making you the most money.

For instance, if you're making the most money from the Yellow Pages, then there's no way for you to double it, so you go to the next one.

If you're making the next most money from a sales letter to upscale neighborhoods, then double the amount that you give out. For example, if you're making $1,100 from 100 letters per week, then you step it up to 200 letters per week. If you're making the most money from Valpak-type ads, then you can put ads in two different zones or two different types, Valpak and Money Maker.

Emphasize referrals even more. Usually you can increase the value if someone sends you a referral. If you normally pay $10 for every referral who becomes a client, then start offering $20 for a limited time. Send a letter to all your clients to tell them about the increased value of a referral for a limited time. Explain to them it's because normally you have a slow season at this time, but if they help you out, you wouldn't have one. In return, you're going to help them out too.

Send out a letter to all of your clients who haven't had their trees pruned or different services done in a year or more. Make sure not to send this to people who have already scheduled tree work or are on a continuity or annual program with you.

This is very powerful: Start at the beginning of your good season or your regular busy season, and all through it, begin to schedule winter work. You're probably terribly busy at this time of year, so schedule things like mistletoe for winter months, and anything that you think would be better in winter months.

Schedule winter work when you may have more clients than you can handle.

Because of the big curve of this business, take some of your clients you think you can do in the wintertime and begin to schedule them at that time. Make a winter month file or winter month callback file. You can offer a slight discount to clients who let you schedule the work in the slow months. Offer a little more discount to encourage prepaying or a deposit. This locks them in.

When I do all these things, my slow season isn't slow at all. Of course, my cost per client rises slightly, but it's still very, very profitable, and many times better than having a slow season.

Remember; start planning months before your slow season starts. Take the proper steps, and then you can laugh at your slow season, symbolically.

It's something that you need to work on now.

In my business, I pay our people to stay with us full time because of the expense of retraining new people. I certainly don't want to lose our good employees.

When you use these marketing strategies, think about it: If you're paying people anyway, even if you made enough profit just to pay the people and pay your light bill and pay things that are going to be paid anyway, then instead of losing money, you've now broken even.

Of course, the ideal is to make profit on it.

If you are not doing any work that day, then you're still going to pay your bills, you're still going to pay for your office staff, you're going to pay for the workers you want to keep on. So any work that you bring in avoids you going in the hole that day.

You at the least break even, or hopefully make more money and profit.

Why do it alone? I've got dozens of low- to no-cost strategies to increase your sales in your normal "slow season" quickly!

Go to www.treecaresuccess.com and sign up for membership in my "Millionaire Maker" Inner Circle Program.

In Closing

All right. Now let's use these strategies to tear into your business structure.

I want to thank you for reading this book. The ideas contained in this program will make you more money and get you more clients if you use them.

What I suggest you do is sit down right now and make a list of your ideas. Then go back through the book again. Each time you go through it, I guarantee you're going to get more ideas.

Some of you will have a lot of success by keeping a notepad by your bedside. That way, when you're thinking, just before going to sleep or just after waking up, you can write down any new ideas that come to mind. Do it immediately because it will set you on the right path quickly.

If you have any questions or comments about the material in this book, just shoot me an email at john@jdavistreecare.com.

A lot of these strategies will be more exhaustively explained in my "Millionaire Maker" Inner Circle Program.

My "Millionaire Maker" Elite Inner Circle Program gives you some tremendous stuff and some tremendous tools that you can use in addition to this program in your business. I go into detail on many of these things. I give you new stuff every month that you can immediately put into play in your business. You can review the details and sign up for a two month FREE trial at *www.treecaresuccess.com.*

Remember that this is an ongoing program. This is a living program. It's not something you just get and it all stops. Through this program, I will help you send your tree care or your landscape business to a much higher level.

Having said that, just give me a call if you have any problems or concerns. Here's to your great success!

Go here **now to get started:**

www.treecaresuccess.com

Copyright 2006. RENEGADE Marketing Systems, Inc. All rights reserved.

Email: John@TreeCareSuccess.com : Address: 225 CR 4594 Boyd, Texas 76023

Appendix A

#1

You've Won a Free Tree Hazard and Health Evaluation

4206 Broadway Ave
Haltom City, TX 76179

Julie Armijo
505 Ryan Street
Saginaw TX, 76179

J Davis TREE CARE SOLUTIONS

Dear Friend,

    This is John Davis, owner of *JDavis* Tree Service. You've won a free tree hazard and health evaluation absolutely free. No strings attached. No teeny, tiny little print. One free evaluation. A coupon is enclosed for you to redeem.

I Miss You!

(turn over)

You've had tree work done by my company before, but you haven't in a while. I miss you.

Don't you remember how your trees looked after we pruned them?

They looked sensational! Manicured. Healthy. Rejuvenated. It was fantastic.

It's been quite a while since you've had your trees pruned. Too long. You know you should but ...

I know, I know you've been meaning to get your trees pruned, but you just haven't taken the time. I'm sure there are plenty of good reasons why you haven't done it.

You are busy. Preoccupied with work and the kids. You're being pulled in sixty-three different directions at once. You're tired. Who has time or the energy to even think about the trees? By the time you get the crisis-of-the-day fixed, you just want to relax. Just a moment of peace. You deserve it. And weekends? Well, they go by so fast it seems like Monday morning is there moments after Friday night left.

Why Am I Giving You a Free Tree Hazard and Health Evaluation?

Due to the severe weather conditions, trees have been weakened, stressed, and badly damaged. Since we have not seen you in a while and you are a valuable customer, we would like to come out and make sure your trees are safe and healthy.

So I chose a few select clients to receive a **free tree hazard and health evaluation**. No strings attached. You don't have to buy anything else. Not one thing. This is a free gift.

How Can I Afford to Do This?

Thank you for being so concerned about me. The truth is that some of my clients will choose to have their trees pruned, removed, or fertilized. Not all, but some. Enough so that I can afford to give this away to a few select clients.

This offer won't last long. After [date not more than forty-five days away], it's all over. The coupon enclosed will expire.

Call me now at (817) 274-TREE (8733) to schedule your **free tree hazard and health evaluation**.

Sincerely,

John Davis
JDavis Tree Care Solutions

P.S. Don't miss out - you've won a FREE **tree hazard and health evaluation**. No strings attached. That's up to a ????? value. You must claim your prize by [date]!

2

JDavis Tree Care Solutions
"The Most Thorough Tree Care *Ever* ... or it's FREE!"
Up to 12 Months to Pay, NO INTEREST!

This past year, we provided a quote to complete tree service at your home, and we never heard back from you. Many of our clients have told us their budget was stopping them from moving forward, so we have arranged an easy payment solution: **_We would do most anything to keep you as a client!!_**

So... please consider our JDavis Tree Care "No-Brainer" Payment Plan

If you want to pay in full, you can take a 13% discount off your ticket.

"0" % Interest !
With Up to 12 MONTHS to Pay
Call for details or to schedule

OR

You decide. It's your choice

But you must call in the next **TEN DAYS**.

Every service is still backed by our **100 percent risk-free guarantee**. Nothing is more important to us than your complete and total satisfaction.

<u>**We take all of the risk. If you are not happy, we will redo any item in question. If you are still not happy, you don't owe us a dime. Not one red cent! No hard feelings.**</u>

We know you are busy and tree care is not the highest priority in your life.

As professional arborists, tree care and health is our specialty and our top priority. We understand that the trees in your landscape need special care to survive and thrive in today's harsh environment. Pollution, insects, disease, and urban sprawl are all enemies to your trees' health.

It's a sad day when a homeowner calls us with that heart-wrenching refrain, ***"We've lived here for years and our tree looked fine, but I looked up one day, and it seemed to be dying! What happened?"***

<u>ANSWER:</u> Pollutants. Herbicides. Weed killers. People activity compacting the soil, restricting oxygen. Turf root competition. Lack of DEEP ROOT fertilization to replace nutrients leached from the soil over time. Deadwood accumulating, stressing the tree and allowing a fatal tree disease to enter over time.

The list goes on.

Why care about your trees' health?

Without trees, life on Earth would be impossible!
<u>Yes, it's a scientific fact that without trees, life on Earth would be impossible!</u> Trees absorb carbon dioxide pollutants and give back oxygen.

Fact 1: *An acre of trees absorbs as much CO_2 as we would produce if we drove a car 26,000 miles (that's around the Earth!).*

Fact 2: *An acre of trees produces enough oxygen for eighteen people to live on for a day.*

It is estimated that one acre of healthy trees can absorb six tons of carbon dioxide and produce four tons of oxygen in just one year!

*(Please read next page for **FREE** zoo tickets)*

Tree leaves give off tremendous amounts of water and cool the air on hot summer days, reducing the temperature in your yard and making it easier to breathe. Trees shield your home from the heat and cold winter winds, resulting in much lower utility bills.

Trees are so common, it's easy to take them for granted and assume that they can exist without our help. Unfortunately, that's not always true for trees in an urban environment. Like any living thing, trees need periodic health care—fertilizing, pruning, and treatments for harmful insects, injury, and disease.

Read the enclosed raving testimonials of our clients

Hundreds of referrals in your area, from your neighbors, available upon request

It's easy to protect your trees; in fact, it involves only two simple steps!
Step 1: Start by calling 817-274-TREE (8733) TODAY, before this offer expires IN TEN DAYS!
Use your previous quote, or schedule another at your convenience. Mention that I sent you this letter, and

I will send you two FREE Ft. Worth Zoo tickets when you schedule your service.

As professional arborists, we are dedicated to helping trees. We provide expert pruning of trees and shrubs for health and aesthetic reasons, fertilize them for strong and healthy growth, protect them from insects and disease, and inspect them regularly so they will continue to enhance the beauty and value of your property.

Step 2: Relax. Let our expert tree care professionals take "The Most Thorough Care of Your Trees *Ever* ... (It's Guaranteed)" and take some time to maybe plant another tree. Remember–the world can't have too many trees. After all, they are one of nature's most amazing creations. I look forward to hearing from you soon.

To your trees' health,

John P. Davis
President

Call 817-274-TREE (8733)

PS: Our new easy payment plans: **Up to twelve easy monthly payments with no INTEREST** or ninety days, same as cash, **NO INTEREST**! Make it easy on your budget to give your trees the very best care they deserve now.

PPS: If you would like to pay in full, take an extra 13 percent OFF your bill!

PPPS: Call Now! This offer only good for the next TEN DAYS or to the first fifty clients who call. Then that's it; Sorry.

#3

J Davis
TREE CARE SOLUTIONS

An urgent message from
John P. Davis, President

Here's a SHAMELESS BRIBE that's worth at least $181 ... perhaps $272 ... or maybe even more ... but only if you shout, "YES—I'll accept your bribe!" and have us care for your trees before Feb. 28th!

Dear tree owner,

Don't let that word "bribe" give you the wrong idea. This is a perfectly legitimate offer. But words like "savings" or "discount" simply aren't powerful enough for this introductory, limited-time, everybody-wins offer! Here's why ...

Your trees—which may be worth thousands of dollars each if you had to replace them—deserve the best care possible. You can't entrust them to some stranger with a pickup truck, a ladder, a chain saw, and little or no tree care knowledge. You need professionals—with a reputation for excellence, dependability, and fair prices ... and with the strongest guarantee in the tree-care industry: **If you're not completely satisfied with our work, there's no charge!**

**We're the professionals: JDavis Tree Care Solutions.
And instead of spending a lot of money on advertising,
to attract new customers, we'd rather *bribe* you!**

Perhaps, during the past twenty years, you've seen some of our crews working on trees in your neighborhood. As one of the largest tree-care service companies in this area, we have a large fleet of trucks, towing tree chippers all around your neighborhood. But that's not all …

Our tree-pruning crews are well-trained, highly professional arborists, climbers, and other tree-care professionals. And they're all well-paid, full-time, year-round employees (not poorly trained, minimum-wage, seasonal employees.) We don't lay them off in the fall … then try to hire and train new crews in the spring. It takes years for tree-care professionals to get the classroom training and on-the-job experience they need. But it's the only way to make sure that your trees are cared for properly.

And that's exactly what we'd like to do: care for your trees properly—right now—so you'll experience our work firsthand and then entrust your trees to us from now on! This is where our bribe comes in. As you might expect, we're busiest during the warmer months. Right now, though, we're not busy all the time. We have a few openings, gaps here and there in our schedule. And rather than have some of our crews sit idle—and instead of spending thousands of dollars on newspaper, radio, or TV ads to attract new customers—we'd rather spend a few dollars on printing and postage to reach tree-owners like you. And to offer a bribe that's worth at least $181 … or significantly more!

How much can you save by accepting our bribe? That depends on which service you want, how many crews or pieces of equipment are needed, and how long it takes. But let's use a typical tree-pruning job as an example. Our regular fee for one hour of work can be as high as $255 —for an entire crew. It's a very fair price for top-quality, guaranteed tree work. But if you call right now, and schedule the work between now and Feb. 28, 2003, we'll charge you ...

**Only $329 for the first two hours—you'll save $181!
Just $164.50 for each additional hour (if any) —
that's almost 40 percent off!
Or, if you would like, two hours is only $27.42 + tax
monthly, <u>NO INTEREST</u>,
conveniently charged to your credit card each
month for twelve months.**

And here's a fact that's suspiciously coincidental, but true, as you'll see when you read the enclosed leaflet. Saving money is not the only good reason to call us today. It just happens to be the best time of the year for pruning! It's a good time, too, for other services, such as tree removal and deep-root fertilization/aeration. What's more ...

* Even with our bribe, there's no drive-time charge! The clock starts running only when our crew arrives at your location—not when they start driving to it.
* If you feel more comfortable with it, we'll bid your job—not just estimate it! We'll look over what needs to be done and submit a bid. After you approve it, that's the full amount we'll bill you ... even if the work takes longer than we figured or it's more difficult than we thought. No

unpleasant surprises! If you don't accept our proposal, **I WILL GIVE YOU $20 COLD CASH** just for your trouble.

* You must be delighted with our work, or we'll redo it until you are. And then, if you're still not completely satisfied, we'll tear up your bill and won't charge you a dime!

* All clean-up work is included, so there's no mess left behind. Or, if you prefer, you can do the clean-up, and our crew will use the time to work on your trees a little longer!

**It's a win-win situation for all concerned!
You save money, and we hopefully gain a long-term client.
Plus, your trees get the expert care they need ...
when they need it!**

So don't miss out on the savings. In order to qualify for the bribe, you must let us know between now and February 28, 2003. And you **MUST** be a new customer. And since you're not the only one we're mailing this offer to, I urge you to call us right now. Who knows? If enough people respond, our slower season might turn into one of our busier seasons. Then you'd have to wait weeks for an appointment...at our regular rates!

Go to your phone right now and give us a call at **817-274-TREE (8733)** *before the deadline.*
Cordially,

John P. Davis, Owner
JDavis Tree Care Solutions

PS: Ask about our "90-day same-as-cash" plan ... or easy monthly payments!

PPS: Some companies charge for bids. I will **PAY YOU $20** just for taking your time to get a bid from us. What a difference!

More Help for Your Business

In the past thirty-seven years of working with some of the world's largest and most successful companies and corporations, as well as hundreds of small and medium-size businesses, the business development consultants of TopLine Business Solutions have been able to uncover tremendous profit centers that have been lying dormant, just waiting to be tapped—ready to unleash a flood of newfound profits that go directly to the business's bottom line.

John Davis, owner of **RENEGADE** Marketing Systems, is a TopLine-trained business consultant. If you're serious about growing your business, virtually eliminating your competition, and dominating your market, we need to talk. The ideas, strategies, and systems we can create for you and install in your business have been proven time and time again in countless businesses, in a variety of industries, and in nearly every profession. And we are confident we can work the same magic for you and your business. The future of your business is directly in your hands. To ensure its success, just pick up the phone and give us a call at **(817) 222-9494.**

We'll be happy to discuss how, together, we can create a powerful marketing strategy that will position your business to become not *only* the obvious choice, but in reality, the only choice for your prospects and customers—and your competition won't stand a chance.

So don't delay. Pick up the phone now and give us a call—before your competition does. We guarantee you won't regret it.

All the Tools, Systems, and Methodology to Give You an Unfair Advantage in Your Marketplace

The principles that make up the **RENEGADE** business building and development systems have been used to make enormous profits for businesses of all sizes and types, and in nearly every business, industry, and profession. **RENEGADE** Marketing, through TopLine, has adapted and refined these principles into a series of dynamic and scientific processes that meet the challenges facing businesses operating in today's highly competitive environment. **RENEGADE** Marketing Systems can help you ...

- Drive hordes of hungry customers to your business.
- Craft and use powerful and irresistible direct-marketing strategies to drive your sales through the roof.
- Counter competitor price-cutting without reducing your margins.
- Keep customers coming back again and again to your business.
- Uncover and profit from the hidden and untapped assets to be found in your business.
- Quickly, simply and effectively increase sales to your current customers by 10, 35, and even 90 percent or more, with no additional marketing costs.
- Advertise your business for absolutely no cost.
- Create passionate and undying customer loyalty to permanently keep your competitors out.
- Find, acquire, keep, and motivate superstar salespeople and employees.

- Live and enjoy greater success by speedily building a business that is highly profitable and will run itself.
- Make your business 100 percent recession-proof in thirty days or less.
- Get and use testimonials to dramatically boost your sales.
- Use price testing to garner maximum profit from every sale you make.
- Add an immediate $5,000 to $10,000 in new-found profits in the next thirty days.
- Double, triple, and even quadruple your sales conversion rate.
- And much, much more ...

John P. Davis
RENEGADE Marketing Systems
Telephone: 817-222-9494
E-mail us at: john@treecaresuccess.com
www.treecaresuccess.com

CPSIA information can be obtained at www.ICGtesting.com
Printed in the USA
BVOW071011260313

316493BV00001B/204/P

9 781434 333537